AMMO GRRRLL RELOADS

Volume 6 2019-2020

ISBN: 978-1-7370167-1-7

Other books by Susan Vass include:

Ammo Grrrll Hits the Target (Volume 1)
Ammo Grrrll Aims True (Volume 2)
Ammo Grrrll Returns Fire (Volume 3)
Ammo Grrrll Is Home on the Range (Volume 4)
Ammo Grrrll Is A Straight Shooter (Volume 5)
Ammo Grrrll Gets Shot (Volume 7)

Other books published by VWAM, LLC include these novels by Max Cossack, in chronological order:

Khaybar, Minnesota
Zarah's Fire
Simple Grifts: A Comedy of Social Justice
Low Tech Killers
Where There Is No Man

DEDICATION – to Heather Beresford (Lattimore)

This book is dedicated to the memory of one of the dearest friends a girl could ever have had: Heather Beresford (Lattimore). Heather was the twin sister of Bonnie, my best friend from age 14, and, of course, a great friend in her own right. In fact, the three of us were so inseparable that several people referred to us as “the triplets”, though sadly, I did not resemble them physically, except in height, or lack of same.

Heather was passionate about everything in her world: books; animals, especially dogs, cats, and horses; conservative / Libertarian politics; her extended family; and her beloved adopted state of Texas. She became an adopted daughter of Texas when she married Lee and moved there. She was rarely without an article of clothing sporting the Lone Star.

She and Lee made a hobby of pilgrimages to various quaint and architecturally lovely County Courthouses. She was beautiful, vivacious, extremely intelligent, compassionate, and loyal to a fault. After nursing husband, Lee, until he passed from COPD, she had the great good fortune to find Bill Lattimore who became the husband she had hoped to live with for many years. They were madly in love and had several years of companionship and fun til she was diagnosed with Stage 4 Lung Cancer that had already spread to her brain. She put up a brave fight but the insidious disease that would later also strike down Rush Limbaugh, took her way too soon.

I think of her virtually every day and miss her fiercely. RIP, dear friend. How I wish you were still with us to help us fight.

Susan Vass
Maricopa, AZ, March 2021

ADDITIONAL THANKS TO:

The four writers who maintain the Power Line Blog site, Scott Johnson, Steve Hayward, John Hinderaker and Paul Mirengoff. These gentlemen have given me the chance to amuse and bloviate every Friday for, lo, these six years now, and counting.

Gratitude also – really the depth of which can scarcely be expressed – to what has grown to be a family of regular commenters. In the first couple of books it was theoretically possible to list most of the super-stars without fear of leaving someone out, but that is no longer possible. "Favorites" now run to a couple of hundred and I would hate to hurt anybody's feelings by inadvertently omitting them.

AMMO GRRRLL – WHAT THE HECK?

Since this is my sixth book, frankly I am tired of explaining how I came to be called Ammo Grrrll. I wrote this explanation for Book 4, *Ammo Grrrll Is Home On The Range*, and I think it is definitive. And so, I am just plagiarizing my own self (again) for this incarnation and maybe all subsequent ones. If you read it in *Ammo Grrrll Is A Straight Shooter*, and remember it, you have my deep respect.

Here it is: After several decades as a standup comic, I retired and moved permanently -- from Minnesota – where I had to go away for several months in the frigid winter -- to Arizona, where I have to go away for several months in the hellish summer. Sadly, in this great and good land, if you happen to find a place with pleasant year-round weather, you can't possibly afford to actually live there.

I have been married for hundreds of years to Joe Vass, also known as famous novelist Max Cossack. He writes gripping and humorous ebooks which can be located and ordered on Amazon and paperbacks which can be ordered from us at VWAM.com.

In 2011, he took up target shooting with a nice Springfield Armory .40 caliber pistol. At first, he could just go down to the local Walmart and buy boxes of ammo right off the shelves. But then during Barack Hussein Obama's reign, suddenly, ammo just dried up. I'm sure it was mostly a coincidence and had nothing to do with the bizarre idea that the Department of Agriculture, to name just one government agency, should have its own SWAT Team and millions of rounds of ammo. Whatever. He's gone now; and at this writing, Donald J. Trump is President and the shelves are once more full of ammo in nice organized stacks.

With ammo in short supply, it became my task to stand in line for many hours a day to secure it. This became a Sacred Quest and a social event and I acquired the nickname "Ammo Grrrll" from the sales people and other customers in line. This continued for a couple of years. Eventually, in March of 2014, I wrote what was a moderately-amusing little column about my experiences in gun-friendly Arizona and fired it off to Scott Johnson, of Power Line to see if he might be interested in a featured piece about the topic every once in a while.

Before I could even go get another cup of coffee, it appeared on the site and -- just like that! -- I was a columnist! It looked like I was never going to have to "Learn to Code" after all! True, there was no money in it, but, fortunately, my husband (the aforementioned Max Cossack, famous novelist), had already Learned to Code and had done pretty well with it.

I could afford to be a Kept Woman, if you count doing cooking, cleanup, laundry, shopping, and housekeeping for about half a century being "Kept".

Having two jobs with the column provides a kind of safety valve for my legendary and professional-level Powers of Procrastination. When I am "supposed" to be writing, I can decide that it is urgent to organize my sock drawer; and when I am "supposed" to be making and freezing appetizers for an upcoming cocktail party, I can tell myself that I better sit down at my computer and write a topical piece about the 29th Democrat candidate for President in 2020 – this one a trans-gendered Samoan who is also 1/1024th Navajo and can prove it with her application to law school in Colorado.

Then, I can actually do neither and just sit and read the newest Lee Child or Robert Crais book and pretend Reacher or Joe Pike is a very special friend of mine. Very special.

ABOUT THE TITLE

The title of this compilation book – *Ammo Grrrll Reloads* – has two meanings, only one of which is applicable to me.

Of course, "reloading" in the common parlance means placing more rounds into your magazine when that magazine is empty – either in the beginning of a target-practice session – or, far less likely, after you have emptied the magazine into some Zombies during the Apocalypse.

But, additionally, "reloading" is the name for the practice of making your own rounds. Although I know several people who do this, I do not reload. I have neither the room for the vast array of equipment and supplies needed to do this – benches, bullets, powder, casings, primers – nor the skill and knowledge that it would take. Technical skills are not my long suit. You might even say that I have a "void" in that suit, which doesn't come in nearly as handy as a "void" does in the card game of Bridge.

People who do reload maintain that you can shoot a lot more rounds for the same price as buying off the rack, and also that you can make custom rounds for every one of your weapons. Good for them, but that is not ever going to be part of the skillset of anyone who lives in this house. I know without a doubt that I would blow us all to Kingdom Come, or at the very least, blow up my favorite gun.

If you are a re-loader, my hat is off to you, and more "powder" to you!

As we cavort through these columns, through the four seasons, you may notice that some of the themes from my previous column compilations seem to re-appear. That is true.

Some evil refuses to die, like the weird bad guys in the Pirates of the Caribbean series.

So, thanks for buying this book and happy reading.

APRIL THRU JUNE

Since I started my columnist job in the last week of March, 2014, each subsequent year of columns begins in April and ends in March of the next year. I shall give you little previews of what's in store, quarter by quarter.

The First Quarter opens with a bang with the sickening news that Hate Crime Hoaxer, Jussie Smollett will not have charges brought against him for the expensive wild goose chase he set off in the beleaguered City of Chicago. It's not like they didn't have enough real crime to pursue. Though he didn't even have to admit that he faked the whole thing, at least the lying little whiner lost his job.

Which segues nicely into a column about my husband's retirement from his day job and his transition to writing action/adventure thrillers as Max Cossack. It is exciting to be married to somebody else after half a century, even though he appears to be wearing the same clothes. No, not JUST the same clothes as Joe Vass; the same clothes he has been wearing for half a century! At least he can do so. I have no fewer than four complete sets of clothing in Laughably Small, Almost Fitting, Pretty Much Fitting, and Despairingly Large. The next column explores the age-old debate: "IS the 'customer always right'? Or can the 'uncomfortable' feelings of a millennial receptionist trump the rights of a long-time customer?"

With all the attacks on everything American, my next piece asks the very logical and timely question "If This Isn't Nice, What Is?"

Which will bring us to May and the tragic death of one of my long-time and best friends. This book is dedicated to Heather and the tribute to her can be found in the May 10th column. It could have been 20 pages, but I was confined to the column's usual format. I will miss her for as long as I live, and we sure will miss her vote next November.

Life goes on, the struggle goes on, the absurd goes on. The next column deals with an actress mother who is allowing her pre-teen child to decide xer gender, and the column after that discusses the world-shaking sex strike by angry women. Shockingly, the country evidently survived the loss of their conjugal cooperation, in fact, barely noticed.

As we head into June, the Democrats do their level best to be the Worst Party Ever, and the President shocks the Left by accurately describing many dreadful unlivable countries as "sh*thole" places. Pearls were clutched; the word "racist" was thrown around a lot even though he never specified that the countries so described were filled with people of color. Uh oh. SOMEbody heard a "dog whistle" that was never blown! Again!

And we leave June and head into the Second Quarter with the first entry from our big six-week Road Trip called "No Mountain For Old Ladies." Enjoy the ride-along.

CHEWING THROUGH MY RESTRAINTS

April 6, 2019

I once saw a joke t-shirt in the Mall that I related to. It said: "Some days it doesn't even seem worth it to chew through my restraints."

I am generally a very happy if somewhat-high strung person. I experience the usual bouts of anxiety and grief over loss and pain as any normal person would, but I try to stay upbeat most of the time. But every once in awhile – certainly not more than twice a day – something is so mind-blowing, so upsetting, that, as the tired expression goes, "I can't even..."

For example, the THIRD bogus Kavanaugh accusation – the letter clearly copied straight from bad porn that had both Kavanaugh and his pal in a car with a woman taking turns doing things nearly anatomically-impossible. The woman later confessed that she made the whole thing up for attention. And we never heard if she suffered the slightest consequence.

It was, after all, no more "un-credible" than the clinically insane idea that a group of high school boys could have regularly scheduled gang-rape parties with spiked punch and drugs and NOBODY – not the "victim" girls nor the proud perps – told a soul. Yes, friends, many many people were alleged to be involved and not one word leaked! For the love of God, sign them up for the intelligence agencies! Those folks leak like an incontinent geezer laughing, coughing, or sneezing! Probably just coughing or sneezing. Those Deep State guys seem to have no sense of humor at all. Well, except for John "Bucket O' Laughs" Brennan.

But millions – MILLIONS – of idiotic women celebrities, keening feminists screeching and scratching on the Supreme Court door, and even a few sorta-men celebrities and activists claimed with straight faces to believe it! “Women must be believed! Women never lie!“

Only a person who has never known a woman or never BEEN a woman believes that. Are YOU a woman reading this right now? Have YOU ever lied? Yeah, me neither. Show me the listed weight on your Driver’s License while standing on a scale. Show me your “Food Log” at Weight Watchers. Let me listen to you tell your dental hygienist how regularly you floss. Let me hear you phone your employer from the beach to say you are sick. Let me see ID on every single person claiming to be celebrating a birthday at any free-birthday dessert restaurant. Just sayin’.

Moving on. We talk a lot about Unity, Reconciliation, Coming Together – black and white, men and women, gays and straights, conservatives and psychotics (haha, I kid the psychotic leftists). And, finally, we may have that issue that brings us all together, Kumbaya style: No, it’s not the tedious “conversation” about race we’ve been hearing about for 60 years.

It’s The Jussie Smollett Obama-Connected Fix Being In. Yeah, it’s old news, but I want to do my part to keep it on the front burner. The judge who sealed the material “accidentally” assures us he can get to the unsealing, probably, by May. In every such corrupt event, the miscreants count on the 3-day Attention Span of the American people. Don’t let it drop!

The cops are livid. Chris Rock, no Republican, mocked Jussie. Even the cast of *Empire* is divided. Obama stalwarts Rahm Emmanuel and David Axelrod at least pretended to be

upset for a couple of minutes before pivoting rapidly and reflexively to "Trump caused it." I don't know when Trump found the time when he was so busy "causing" the New Zealand massacre. Is there anything that guy can't do?
I have to admit to being stunned by the Jussie outcome. I have lived long and seen many amazing things. I generally feel immune to being shocked or blindsided about anything. But this really took the cake. Sixteen counts, an absurd, evolving tale that stunk from Day One, and proof positive that the little racist me-monster arranged the whole hoax.

And he walks! Friends of friends make a few phone calls and the problem disappears for Jussie. That's some kind of friends! Who has that kind of juice? Rachel, Brian, Morning Joe, Van, Ana? Calling all "journalists"! Here's a real poser for you to investigate. Hey, you might even be able to recycle some of your "Collusion" chyrons!

If I were the Chicago PD, I would release every SCRAP of evidence against Jussie. Stand in a solid phalanx thousands strong in uniform while passing out the information to random passersby – have it dropped from Police helicopters — and DARE some corrupt black robe and the whole DA's office to arrest you all, if they can find a law enforcement agency to do so.

I bet 98 percent of Americans will agree with me when I say that I have no interest whatsoever in seeing this narcissistic little hate-monger spend a lot of time in jail at taxpayer expense. What I want is for him to have to CONFESS on television that he committed the hoax and apologize to all white people, especially MAGA supporters.

And then, since at least one of his motives – besides the standard Trump-hatred and racist white-hatred – was to get attention and leverage for a higher salary, I want a SUBSTANTIAL fine that would actually hurt. Heck, he can always have a GoFundMe campaign in which Soros and all the celebrity haters who bought and spread the original preposterous tale can pitch in. But he should not be able to claim "vindication" and even yak about suing the police department.

Ya basta. Enough! Since I wrote part of this column a good while back near St. Patrick's Day, I end with a limerick. Pour yourself a morning beer — okay, a Mimosa — and enjoy.

For most people, black, brown or white
Whose criminal acts come to light
Our friends in low places
Can't dismiss our cases
When the Grand Jury votes to indict.
But Jussie isn't just black,
He also likes men in the sack,
He committed a crime
But will not do his time
Cuz Obama and friends got his back.

MARRIED TO AN ENTHUSIAST

April 12, 2019

We are now in our tenth year of living in Arizona. Before that we "wintered" in San Diego for two years and then Palm Springs for ten. I would notice groups of men lingering over coffee in the upscale supermarket. These were married retirees, men who had clearly been kicked out of their small winter condos by wives who probably loved them dearly but desperately needed some solitude, some "space." (I suppose it is also possible that the men were just as happy to escape briefly from their wives, but in my experience, men can just turn up the television and pretend we aren't even there. Hypothetically.)

A friend has a pillow in his office, a needlepointed message that says bluntly: "Retirement means half the income and twice the husband."

I would sometimes see the coffee drinkers check their watches to see if they were allowed to go home yet. (This was a few years before cellphones when we can all be alone with our new BFF, Alexa, and amuse ourselves into solitary oblivion, even out to dinner in a group.)

My husband – the famous novelist Max Cossack – retires this Friday! Since we have both been either self-employed or working from home for decades, I will not have to adjust to his being around.

But neither will I need to fix him up with playdates with other men to golf or walk or just sit around SOMEWHERE ELSE, FOR GOD'S SAKE. Max is the most self-amusing human I have ever known, mostly due to an overabundance of enthusiasms and boundless curiosity about every dang thing in the world. Sometimes, possibly, to a fault.

He is a voracious reader who will pick up *War and Peace* or *Moby Dick* just for a little light reading. And then he will read seven books about Whale Oil, Ship Construction, or biographies of Herman Melville or Leo Tolstoy. He loves biographies and has read either biographies or autobiographies of, among many others, such unlikely subjects as Shania Twain and Keith Richards. Yes, really.
Unlike me, he also loves television. We once got a cable baseball package with which he could watch up to ten games a day. He has watched documentaries about wars, Presidents, and also everything he ever wanted to know about Bananas, and the Histories of Ice Cream, Chocolate, and Corn Flakes. He can go on about any of these subjects at some length, even in the unlikely event that there are no requests.

Recently he became enamored with Teddy Roosevelt and we took a summer trip to see various Teddy-related parks and sites in North Dakota and Montana. As is my wont, I will tell loyal readers about what diners and restaurants we found on the way, and everything I ate. That is more my speed.

While working full-time, Max attended Night Law School, graduating 5th in his class. He also composed and recorded dozens of pieces of music and wrote 4 musicals and plays, all of which were actually produced! (If you are not in or around the theater, you have no idea how unusual that is.) And in the last year or so, he researched and wrote two outstanding novels. It would not surprise me if – free at last, free at last, thank God A'mighty, he's free at last – he produces a novel every six weeks now in retirement. Please buy them so we can buy more ammo.

Remember when Valerie Jarrett told us that Barack Hussein Obama was bored all the time because he was just so dang much smarter than the rest of us? Alas, she had confused boredom with sheer laziness and lack of imagination. It's a common mistake.

My experience with the very smart people it has been my privilege to know is that the very smart – not at all to be confused with the merely "edumacated" — are almost NEVER bored, unless stuck in an airport with CNN shrieking hatefully at them. If they max out on one thing, the very smart will just go ahead and teach themselves another language or learn to crochet or fly a plane or design a giant model railroad or make their own ammo or make a spreadsheet inventorying all their ammo, or manage their Fantasy Baseball Teams or do Mensa-level Sudoku with math involved.

My former "yard guy," with his 5th grade formal education, could fix anything. He had a very hard life, but was always joyful and grateful. He sang to the plants! He was lightyears smarter than almost any talking head on television prattling on about whatever talking point memo the DNC put out that morning. Hey, kids, is it "the beginning of the end" again, or are the "walls closing in"? Are we Nazis today or in the pocket of Putin? Idiots!

Perhaps it is a mercy on the part of the Lord to make the dull-witted also short on self-awareness so that they don't get embarrassed when they say things like that there is no difference between the Berlin Wall – which, of course, kept imprisoned people IN, and the Gaza Wall, which keeps vile terrorists OUT. Or rail against "tactile" nuclear weapons. Luckily, the terminally-stupid often have extreme arrogance to compensate for minimal brains.

I admit to a certain bias here, but I also believe that most really smart people also have highly-developed senses of humor. Even if they can't tell jokes – and most can – they "get" them. This is why almost the entire current crop of standup "comics," whose shtick consists mostly of either filling a checked Diversity box or saying obscene things about the President and his family, are not funny. They are not funny because they do not "think" funny; most do not think at all until they get their "Orange Man Bad" marching orders. I can say categorically that any random Commenter on Power Line is funnier than the entire stable of horrible late-night talk show host comics. (Notable and clean, hilarious exceptions well worth checking out are Brian Regan, Jim Gaffigan, Demetri Martin, and Nate Bargatze.)

I think most very smart people are also joyful, happy to be alive in such an interesting world. Can you even begin to imagine how tedious it must be to be in a relationship with the wretched crop of angry, entitled, spittle-emitting, miserable boring haters that populate all of cable and network television, Hollywood, and most of Twitter? What sane man could even look at a wife dragging around a bloody beheaded likeness of another human being, let alone the President?

WHEN CULTURAL NORMS COLLIDE

April 19, 2019

For a brief time in my comedy career, I was part of a group that conducted Customer Service Training for companies. One of my colleagues told a story which may have been apocryphal and which I can only dredge up from dim 25-years-old memory.

One of the things that will unhinge customers the fastest is being told when making a reasonable request: “That is not our policy.” The example used claimed that a man went into a large business complex which also housed his long-time bank. Since the bank was on the lower floor, he went into the bank to have his parking ramp ticket validated. The cashier said, “It is not our policy to validate tickets when you have not conducted business within the bank.” He argues with her, at first calmly, but with increasing anger. A supervisor is called over who agrees that “it is not our policy.”

Finally, the guy grabs a withdrawal slip and closes his account – to the tune of several hundred thousand dollars – and then asks, “Would this count as a ‘transaction within the bank’?” The clerk agrees that it would and validates his $5.00 parking ticket. Though the anecdote was amusing, illustrative of the point, and clearly meant to be a cautionary tale, I doubted at the time that it had actually happened. Now I’m not so sure…

A friend of mine – a libertarian rancher from Montana, named John – is a fearless defender of important cultural community norms. Two brief examples: He is nearly 80 years old — a fit, but not imposing guy. Once, when he was on his back road, he spotted four young men in a vehicle merrily pitching beer bottles out the window. He pulled over, got out of his car and confronted the miscreants. "Please go pick up your trash," he said. The young men first fell back on the old "What's it to ya?" He answered that it concerned him because it was his road in his beautiful community and he cared. The guys then mulishly agreed to "do it on our way back," but he said, "You'll do it now."

They neither drove away nor shoved him aside, probably because on some level they knew they were in the wrong. Now in Montana as in Arizona they also may have assumed that this old guy could very well be both crazy and armed. But, generally speaking, littering is not considered a capital crime even by the most militant anti-litterers. So, probably, the cultural norm "Don't Litter" plus "Respect your Elders" trumped even their drunken stupidity. They picked up their trash. Community and cultural standards prevailed.

On another occasion, this same gentleman, who had recently sustained a temporarily-disabling injury, arrived for Sunday brunch with friends at the favorite local restaurant only to find the Handicapped Parking slot taken up by one of a row of Harleys! Again, he approached the 5 leather-clad obvious bikers at the bar and asked, "Who's the handicapped biker?"

The guilty biker quickly took his point, mumbled something about not having seen the sign, and trudged out to move his bike. All of us have been tempted on a rainy day to limp away from a convenient Handicapped spot, but most of us don't. We are reluctant to risk a substantial fine, but we also recognize the innate fairness of reserving close-in spots for the genuinely impaired. We believe the cultural norm, "It's fair to accommodate people."

A central tenet of doing any kind of retail or service business is "The customer is always right." My father, owner of a drugstore in a small town, phrased it "The customer may not always be right, but he is always the customer." He did not waste any time on the kind of costly Customer Service Training my friends and I later provided. As I recall, the 3- or 4-minute orientation session when I was 14 went something like this:

"If you don't ask a customer 'May I help you?' within 15 seconds of her entering the store, you will be fired. Treat every customer with courtesy at all times, no exceptions, or you will be fired. Under no circumstances should you ever ask a customer what a product he seeks is for or where it goes – he just might tell you! If a man asks to speak to the druggist and not a teenage girl, come get me; he probably wants rubbers. Keep an eye on older ladies who hover around the wrinkle cream. For some reason, that is one of the few things that people ever steal." He then taught me to count back change into the customer's hand and that was that. As you can imagine, we were all eager not to lose a job in which we made 75 cents each and every hour on the job! Not even to mention the 10 percent discount on cosmetics!

Fast forward now, back to Bozeman, MT and my friend. His working ranch is just outside the limit for daily delivery of the Wall Street Journal. It arrives by mail at his place several days late. For that reason, he sometimes would visit his investment company office at end of his long ranch day to look at the neatly-folded Journal set aside specifically for customers.

At some point, the young receptionist there asked for a "sit-down" with her boss and my friend (the long-time customer) because she felt "uncomfortable" when he came in with almost nobody else around. He had never spoken a word to her outside of the most basic of pleasantries. He was shocked, offended, and more importantly, scared to death. What comes after "discomfort"? A bogus charge that he verbally abused or touched her? A demand for a pay-off lest she ruin his life? After all, a woman must be believed at all times if she complains about a non-Democrat (not that she asserted any impropriety outside of her "discomfort").

It costs five times as much to get a new customer as it does to keep an old one. Yet a common cultural norm – "the customer is a treasured entity" – has been supplanted by some vague and dangerous notion that at all times young people and especially women are entitled to be "comfortable." On campus, students are guaranteed never to have their delicate ears assaulted by unfamiliar opinions. Should an unwanted opinion somehow sneak by, the professionally offended are entitled to scream, swear and shout down the speaker before retreating to Safe Spaces worthy of preschoolers rather than adults entitled to vote.

We regular workaday folks have felt relatively insulated from the worst of the totalitarian hysteria on campus. But Academia provides a conveyor belt of terrible ideas straight into corporate America. For now, there are other investment firms to which one can take one's considerable assets. But for how long? The day when the vaguely accused can be "branded" as pariahs and refused service elsewhere cannot be far behind. What then? Re-education camps? Gulags? Or just forced to purchase Discomfort Liability Insurance?

On that happy note, I go now to finish prep for the eight days of Passover. Happy Passover to our Jewish readers and a Happy and Blessed Easter to our Christian friends.

IF THIS ISN'T NICE, THEN WHAT IS?

April 26, 2019

On this, the seventh day of Passover, in this Sweet Land of religious Liberty, I look out the window of my modest home in Gated Geezerville, and what do I see?

Well, first of all, it is almost 100 degrees out (in April) and yet my home is cool and comfortable. How Arizona was even settled BEFORE air conditioning will forever be a mystery to me. My dear Mama of blessed memory talked often about the farm in the Dust Bowl in South Dakota with no rain, no running water, locusts, and horrible heat. Though the three children were tasked with dusting every single day, dust still accumulated on every surface, on every windowsill, sometimes measured in inches. It was miserable, yes, and went on for YEARS, but it wasn't 119 degrees.

I have just returned from my human-sized family grocery, Bashas, where I was able to find – at insanely-reasonable prices – such exotic goods as parsnips, papaya, bananas from Honduras, watermelon from Mexico, sweet onions from Hawaii, and pink grapes from Peru. The Kings of Europe had never tasted any of these things. Parsnips, maybe.

If I want another cup of coffee, I go to my Keurig, spin the little cup carousel to select which brand I want – we even have a separate decaf carousel for those who prefer a pointless beverage – press a button, and in less than a minute have a pretty good cup of coffee.

Should I break a tooth, as I have been doing with tedious regularity – pizza crust! Fortune cookie! Pecan? Seriously?

— one phone call will get me seen that very day by my wonderful all-lady dental team about a mile away. Should the break be bad enough, I may have to drive 20 miles into "town" to the oral surgeon. Yes, it will be expensive even with insurance, but that's one of the reasons we have savings. Teeth, it turns out, are really quite important. Which you definitely notice when they start disappearing.

As I believe I have referenced in a previous rant, a friend who winters in Mesa finally tired of hobbling around on her bad hip, bit the bullet and called a surgeon. She was seen the next day, scheduled for surgery the day after that, and a week from the day she called, was walking around in less pain than before the surgery, and doing rehab. A Canadian friend in Palm Springs, prisoner of the great "Medicare for All" in Canada, was in unspeakable hip pain for TWO YEARS before he made it to the top of the queue for surgery. He got a phone call and had one week to make arrangements to get back to Canada for the surgery or lose his place in the queue. And that didn't mean that he'd fall to NEXT in line. Oh heck no, that meant he went to the end of the line again.

Moving right along, should we want to get some entertainment – without even leaving home! — we have several alternative sources wherein every single television program that has ever aired is available, as well as every movie and YouTube of most comedians and music. Not even to mention what's available on our phones and the Internet. As a last resort, of course, there's always TALKING to each other. Naaah. Just kidding.

I could go on, of course, listing blessings of modern life. We haven't even touched Interstate Highways, air travel, deodorant, or indoor plumbing. So, here's the $64,000 question: WHY, FOR HEAVEN'S SAKE, ARE SO MANY PEOPLE ENRAGED ALL THE TIME???

If this isn't nice, then what is?

I would love to bring back a gay man from a century ago and tell him, "Guess what? You can get married now." "I know. I was married." "No, I mean to another man." Dead faint. When he is revived, he hears: "But, listen, some horrible Christian won't bake you a cake with two little plastic guys on top. Sure, you could go to a gay baker or an atheist baker, and probably even get a cake with the little plastic guys actually engaging in sex on the cake, but we have found ONE bakery that won't cooperate and it must be driven out of business."

It would be so great to see the look on the face of a black woman from 1859 when told by a spittle-spraying college freshman today that "Yes, I am at Yale with 400 fewer points on my SATs than the Chinese guy who had to go to Enormous State University, and yes, I have a free ride even though my parents are upper middle class, but I am screaming here today and swearing at my white professor because she said it was no big deal if students wear a Hallowe'en costume that I do not approve of. Also, I think she wears hoop earrings."

Doesn't the very concept of a "microaggression" indicate that there is almost nothing left to protest? In fact, the level of screaming rage seems to be INVERSELY proportional to the seriousness of the pretend offense. So, why do I think the Left has gone psychotic all out of proportion to any real or imagined grievance:

□ It pays. If you don't have nepotism to fall back on – Mika, Chelsea, Meghan, whatever Valerie Jarrett's daughter's name is, I don't care enough to look it up — you're going to need an angle to get spectacularly rich when you know noth-

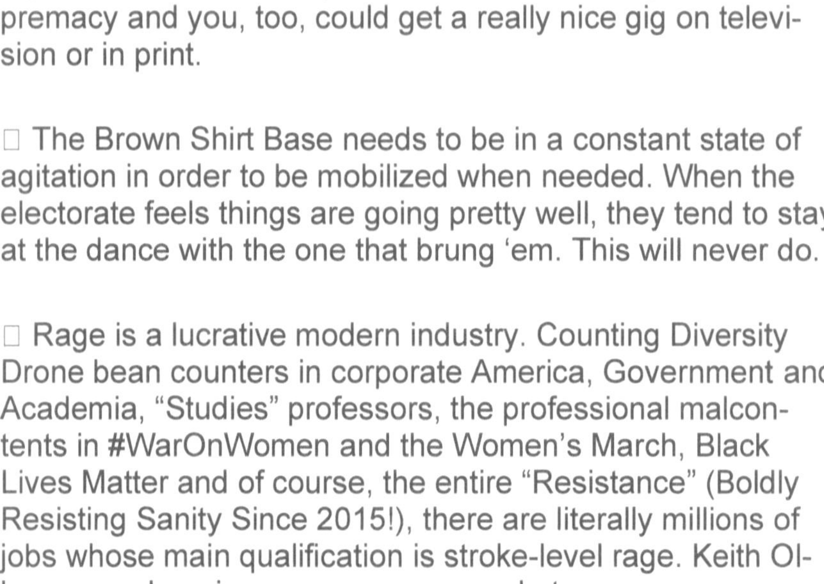

ing and can do less. Yap about toxic masculinity or white supremacy and you, too, could get a really nice gig on television or in print.

- The Brown Shirt Base needs to be in a constant state of agitation in order to be mobilized when needed. When the electorate feels things are going pretty well, they tend to stay at the dance with the one that brung ‘em. This will never do.

- Rage is a lucrative modern industry. Counting Diversity Drone bean counters in corporate America, Government and Academia, “Studies” professors, the professional malcontents in #WarOnWomen and the Women’s March, Black Lives Matter and of course, the entire “Resistance” (Boldly Resisting Sanity Since 2015!), there are literally millions of jobs whose main qualification is stroke-level rage. Keith Olbermann alone is a one-man rage racket.

Therefore, it behooves us to commit a revolutionary act and BE HAPPY. Don’t just “pursue” happiness, as is our God-given right in this great and good country, CATCH happiness and spread it. But, just in case this whole Pollyanna thing doesn’t work out, also buy a gun. Maybe two. Take a safety course, and practice, practice, practice.

THINGS ARE NOT ALWAYS WHAT THEY SEEM

May 3, 2019

So we just had Passover, right? And we went through five boxes of matzo. I make a dish that is kind of like a Passover Lasagna with the matzo playing (badly) the role of the pasta in the layered chicken-mushroom-egg dish. This requires me to break the matzo into various sizes in order to fit in the dish. No problem. Matzo is literally FILLED with little perforations. Ah, but not so fast. For whatever reason, it will never break ON the perforation, no matter what. Because things are not always what they seem. At least, it triggered the theme for this column.

Some comic or pundit many years ago said that if a Martian visited our planet and observed people walking their dogs, that the Martian would conclude that Earth had a race of princely four-legged creatures who kept two-legged slaves whose purpose was to pick up their excrement by hand and deposit it in little bags. To keep the two-legged pooper-scoopers from running off, they were tethered to their masters by long leashes. Anyone who has ever been or known a dog owner would acknowledge that the mistaken characterization of who was slave and who was master was not all that far off the mark.

I was put in mind of that little quip last summer when we visited our investment entity on a very hot day in Arizona. (Def.: any day from mid-April through the end of October). Every millionaire or “many-thousandaire” geezer visiting his or her investments was dressed in large plaid shorts or “breathable” fabric sweat pants, while the attractive young employees of the firm, from receptionists to advisors, were decked out in lovely suits and ties, or high heels and sleek dresses.

It made me laugh out loud. Here is someone in an Armani suit; there is someone in a Spring Training t-shirt and Stein-Mart shorts. See if you can identify the one who has the most money!

Because things are not always what they seem!

For another example, you might think that the New York Yankees – who came very late to the party of putting black people in their precious pinstripes – were incensed about racism wherever it might rear its ugly head, even 80 years ago. But no.

The disgrace of the New York Yankees and Philadelphia Flyers in attacking a dead war bond-raising icon for a stupid song she sang in 1930 has been dealt with brilliantly by both John Hinderaker and dozens of astute commenters who made the point that neither sports club gives a rat's patootie that Kate Smith covered an obscure song about "darkies," a song the black Communist activist Paul Robeson also covered. What they really hate in their heart of hearts are both America and worshipping God in more or less equal portions.

The tedious "racism" charge, routinely flung like poo in a zoo, provides cover for all manner of authoritarian evil just as "anti-Zionism" provides cover for acceptable – yea, mandatory in Leftist circles — hatred of Jews. It's as transparent as Mitt Romney's insane jealousy that Trump accomplished what Mitt could not – winning the Presidency.

I cannot say as the late torch singer, Edith Piaf, allegedly said near the end of her life, "Je ne regrette rien" – I regret nothing." I regret several times that I hurt people's feelings or failed to be my best self. And I wish I could get a do-over on my youthful commitment to leftist idiocy. But one thing I REALLY regret is voting for both John McCain and Mitt Romney. Not that their opponents were preferable. At the time I understood the simple concept of a "binary" choice and did what I could to prevent Obama's reign. Neither vote mattered a fig; I should have just stayed home. And it all turned out EXACTLY as I had expected.

I keep thinking that at 72, I have had all the naiveté beaten out of me by the disappointing behavior of some of my fellow humans. A friend of mine once said that a "cynic" is really just a severely disappointed idealist. Because, on some level, I must still expect that people will act with a modicum of decency and integrity. When John McCain CAMPAIGNED on repealing Obamacare and then delivered the death blow personally to its repeal, with such evident glee at stabbing President Trump in the back, I can honestly say I was surprised. As the old saying goes, "Fool me once, shame on you; fool me 500 times, it's entirely possible that I am an idiot." (Or words to that effect.)

And the unseemly and absurd attack on our beleaguered President by Migrant Mitt with his Carpetbag makes me deeply sorry that I defended him, gave him money, and voted for him. With Arizona's Dynamic Duo of Depressing Divas, Flake and McCain, gone, and even Susan Collins and Lindsey Graham playing shocking heroic roles in the Kavanaugh hearings, there was clearly an opening for Nauseating GOP Turncoat.

Congratulations, Mr. Romney. I think you will beat out even John Kasich for the prize, and that's a pretty high bar. You do know, don't you Mitt, that you will NEVER be President? NEVER. I mean, like, AFTER Hillary. Who will also never be President. The Trump base loathes you, as well we should, and Democrats, who will laud you as "Maverick 2.0" when you are attacking conservatives, will never vote for a rich white Mormon man who isn't at least a transgender communist. Probably by 2024 even declaring that you are moving to Dearborn, converting to Islam, and have always been a woman could not save you. Remember when you were a dog-torturer, unlicensed 14-year-old barber who cut a (maybe) gay guy's hair? Oh, and also gave that woman cancer on purpose? That's just their warm-up act.

So all this narcissistic psychodrama will do you no good. Just stop with the daily flagrant attacks on decency. You met with a "Palestinian" in the Middle East, but not Netanyahu? The rules for this blog prevent me from adequately expressing my dismay. Just think "Robert DeNiro at the Oscars" and then pretend you're not a losing loser who lost and sub in your name for the President's and you'll be in the ballpark.

HEATHER

May 10, 2019

My mission as delineated by my excellent editor and friend, Scott, is both to help him with his self-defined anger management problem and to entertain. So I always feel guilty when I fail to entertain. Sometimes it just can't be helped. Today is such a day.

There is no other way to say it: Delightful regular commenter Heather Beresford fought a brief, courageous battle with an aggressive Stage 4 cancer that had spread from her lungs to her brain, and passed away on April 26, 2019. Her beloved twin sister, Bonnie (Ladyhawk), her wonderful new husband, Bill, and I – and all of us in Heather's large circle of friends and relatives and our commenter Family – have lost a world-class friend. The loss to those of us privileged to have known her well is pretty close to unbearable.

As a corporate speaker/entertainer for a few decades, I often opened with comedy before introducing The Big Deal Credentialed Speaker. Sometimes the credits they insisted I read in the overblown introduction stretched to three or four boring pages – degrees, honors, awards, and plaudits up the wazoo. But rarely did those three pages tell us anything about the character of the person who had earned the degrees. Yet the character of that person was often on display.

Some speakers would have contracts with page after page of "riders" like "I need to wash my hair two hours before the event in Evian water." Or, "I will need a bowl of M & Ms in the green room with all the red ones picked out." Or, "I require a limo ride the 200 feet from my hotel to the event center. I will not shake hands with any audience members at the rope line and I will leave to get the limo back to my hotel 3 minutes after my six-figure speech." Hillary's "riders" and demands were notorious, for example. Raise your hand if you're surprised.

One famous speaker whom I shared a stage with in Pueblo, Colorado, for a women's event would not even ride in the limo they provided for us because it was too old and "germ-filled" and she insisted on a brand new Cadillac off the lot to be schlepped around in. She also refused the nice flower-filled speakers' suite the modest little Super 8 had made by combining two rooms and demanded to be taken instead to the private HOME of the hospital CEO whose hospital was sponsoring the event.

Why do I mention this? Because Heather's CV would not have run to 3 or 4 pages, but she had more character in her little finger than most of those credentialed or celebrated folks have in their entire beings. I believe she had a B.A. from the University of Minnesota. She also earned a certification in a specialty in the aerospace industry rather late in life for which she studied very hard while working full-time and caring for her late husband fighting COPD.

If that doesn't demonstrate enough "character," try this. When Heather was first diagnosed with this wretched, evil disease, it was in early March, just before three separate groups of relatives booked consecutive stays at our casita. Heather hesitated to tell me about her diagnosis because she was afraid it might "spoil my fun" with my relatives. THAT kind of character and selflessness is what I am talking about. The mind boggles.

I first met Heather in 9th grade Social Studies where, due to the happy coincidence of our having last names beginning with "B," she sat behind me. She was an adorable young lady, smart as a whip, with a terrific sense of humor and a raucous, ready laugh. I actually kind of worshiped her, in that Platonic way that young Nerd Grrrlls often are in awe of the more socially-successful girls. Plus, she came with a terrific bonus — an identical twin, Bonnie! – with whom I actually became even closer due in part to the fact that Heather was “cooler” and more self-confident than either of us at that time.

The twins were somewhat exotic to me in that they had moved to Alexandria from Canada, which it turns out, is an entirely different country from ours with weird money and everything. They drank TEA instead of coffee. They watched and understood hockey and cared not a whit for baseball, if you can imagine such a thing when the Minnesota Twins were a brand-new exciting franchise with Harmon Killebrew and Camilo Pascual! Sometimes they even ended their sentences with “eh.”

Their mother, whom I also adored, had been determined from their birth to keep them as individuals, not naming them typical “twin” names like Cindy and Mindy, dressing them differently, and the like. And INDIVIDUALS they both were. In spades. A lot of people we meet kind of remind us of other people we have met, but not these women.

We have known each other for just shy of 60 years, through several husbands (well, I only got the one, but they made up for it), tough times, differing political outlooks for a while, and vast geographical separation. As a blessing in the last decade or so, we became as close again as we had been in high school. I wouldn’t have traded a day of it for all the tea in China and Canada put together. I loved Heather right down to the marrow of my bones and will miss her every day.

Bonnie is still here. She was a godsend to Heather in her hours of greatest need, and is an invaluable surrogate-daughter to my Daddy in Alexandria, Minnesota, and my Best Friend Forever. Bonnie and I discussed our intentions to “live twice as loud” to make up for the years of life missing for Heather. She would like that.

We will also miss Heather’s vote in 2020. Unlike me, she never for a minute flirted with the claptrap that was ’60s left-ism. She was kind, loyal, generous to a fault, witty and wise and madly in love with her new husband, Bill. She made online friends with several Power Line commenters and was a devoted reader and prolific commenter.

When Fridays come and I don’t see her name among the commenters that will be a certain sign that this tragedy really happened and I will have to move on from Denial to another stage of grief. As a wise new friend gently pointed out, for those of us who do not die young, it falls to us to miss and mourn the ones who do. Tough duty. But an honor to do so. For those who don’t think 72 is young, well, you are mistaken. Particularly in the case of this youthful, fun-loving delight of a woman.

I read once that the final words (generally unpublished I would guess) on most “black boxes” recovered from airline crashes are “Oh, sh*t”. Unseemly though that is, that’s how I feel, too, from this tragedy leaving a hole in my world. Call your friends and tell them how much they mean to you while you still can. Leave no love unexpressed.

TODDLERS KNOW BEST

May 17, 2019

The very pretty, fairly talented actress Charlize Theron has informed her public that both her adopted black children are girls. Fair enough. Well, ONE of those little children, now about 7, started out life as a boy child. But when he was three years old – yes, THREE — he came to her and informed her that he was NOT a boy. And that's all it took for him to continue life as a girl. Whatever.

I understand. When our son was 3, he also had an epiphany. We had just moved into our latest in a series of small, cramped apartments, this one on the East Side of St. Paul. This one happened to be a basement apartment. It contained a living room, a teeny tiny bedroom for him, and a second bedroom that could just barely contain our Queen-size bed and dresser. One bathroom between the two bedrooms. The "European" Kitchen (think Romania) featured a spacious Formica counter that came pre-sticky and ran well over 18 inches long, a double sink, a small stove and fridge, both appliances in a festive green color called "Avocado" because it sounds more appealing than "Bile." Do I have to tell you it was the '70s?

Anyway, our imaginative little boy walked into his new digs, noticed that we were partially underground and informed us, "This is a monkey cave, and we're all monkeys in this cave. I am a monkey boy named Chip Chip." He pointed to his father and declared his name to be "Bobo." In an apparent premonition of things to come, he named me "Shot Shot."

Naturally, being extremely WOKE parents who understood that toddlers know best, we immediately began a program of massive reconstructive facial surgery to get him to look as much like a monkey as possible. We also removed his opposable thumbs and marinated him daily in Minoxidil in the hopes of his growing fur. If Precious SAYS he's a monkey, then, by God, he is one and has always been one.

Oh, wait. Now, I remember. We didn't do ANY of that. And lucky for us that we didn't. Because after a few weeks of using our monkey names as a lark, he tired of the game. One day, I said "Chip Chip your lunch is ready" — Grubs and Lice Casserole with 16 bananas — and he looked at me like I had lost my mind and said, "My name is Jacob." And that was that.

A few years ago there was a minor uptick of little African children being adopted by rich, famous white actresses. I have no idea how that will all turn out, but I have no reason to doubt that the ladies' hearts were in the right place. But having a child of color is so yesterday. Now there are at least four actresses claiming one of their children is a transgender. It's one thing when Chaz Bono decides as an adult to do whatever he did to turn from Chastity to Chaz. I wish him nothing but happiness and rooted for him on "Dancing With the Stars" even though he seemed to have all the raw dancing ability of the Hamm's Bear. No worries. I am a lousy dancer too and my husband, the famous novelist Max Cossack, has declared himself to be "the worst dancer that ever lived." I have no reason to doubt his boastful claim.

Adults will do what adults will do. But there is no way on God's green earth that a three-year-old has ANY idea of what his sex is or should be. And in my opinion, despite some insane countries like Canada mandating that "misgendering" one's own children is "violence" and actionable, it borders on child abuse to encourage it.

Here is the Ammo Grrrll recommended response when your three-year-old boy tells you he is NOT a boy. "Yes, you definitely are a boy and it's a GREAT thing to be! There is not one thing that a boy can't do that a girl can. Boys can do and be anything they want – soldiers, carpenters, florists, police officers, fire fighters, farmers, astronauts, hair dressers, baseball players, video game designers, anything you can think of that looks like fun to do, boys can do it! And among the greatest of things that boys can be is to grow up and be Daddies and have wonderful little boys like YOU and wonderful little girls like your baby sister!"

Now why in the world did Ms. Theron not give a speech more or less like that instead of dressing him in girls' clothes going forward? Well, first of all, she has no husband or even "partner" who is male to make the little boy feel special. Put another way, in the words that all the chronic whiners always use when they feel like they are "marginalized" — the little boy had "no one who looked like him" as a role model.

This has always struck me as a particularly stupid statement in a world of truly terrifying levels of stupidity. When I decided to try standup comedy, my "role models" were Bob Newhart, Jack Benny, Woody Allen, The Smothers Brothers, Minnie Pearl, and Joan Rivers, not one of whom looked much like me, even though two of them had lady bits. I learned from their SKILLS and timing, not their genitalia. But, as usual, I digress.

If this little boy watched much television, especially sitcoms and commercials, he would see that grown men are too stupid to live and are always taking orders and rolled-eye advice from their "betters": namely, wives and even, often enough, their precocious, mouthy children.

If this little boy's Mama had the television tuned to anything but Fox News Business, he would hear an absolutely endless stream of hateful drivel about men and masculinity. What little boy wants to be "toxic" even if he doesn't know what the word means? Just by the by, he will also hear tons of racist anti-white crap which could get awkward when his Mama is white.

This little boy dressed in girls' clothing at seven is, for now, living in a make-believe world. It is easier to pretend to be a girl before puberty hits and the Hormones of Craziness kick in totally against our will. Those hormones will determine whether or not we are going to have emotionally-overwrought times of the month, or embarrassing semi-permanent pants protuberances that prevent any desire to go up to the blackboard to show off our math skills.

The hormones will eventually be pretty definitive. What sane person lets a three-year-old make critical life decisions? Heck, Phyllis "Mama Doc" Kahn (D-former MN State Rep for Life) thought 12-year-olds should vote. Well then, why shouldn't six-year-olds get Drivers' Licenses and toddlers choose their own "genders."

And I repeat the mantra I use more frequently all the time: "Thank God I'm pretty old. Maybe I won't have to see my beautiful country take its final degenerate dive over the cliff."

EDITOR'S NOTE: Ilhan Omar defeated 22-term incumbent state representative Phyllis Kahn in the August 2016 DFL primary that augured worse to come. By contrast with Omar, Ms. Kahn is a gracious, straightforward, old-fashioned DFL scrapper. She looks better to me every day.

HARRIDANS ON SEX STRIKE

May 24, 2019

Many current actresses and has-been harridans in Hollywood are registering their shock and fury at losing the sacred and unrestricted right to kill unborn babies in Georgia and Alabama by threatening to withhold sexual favors until the fetal heartbeat law is repealed.

Never mind that for several of them – Bette Midler and the unhinged Rosanna Arquette come to mind – getting pregnant is a ship that has sailed some time ago. Ah yes, but what about their grown daughters' "reproductive rights"? Yeah, what about that? "Reproductive rights" is a repulsive, Orwellian euphemism for something which involves no reproduction whatsoever, only death. How can any woman advocate for the "right" of her daughter to terminate with extreme prejudice her own grandchildren? Beats me.

But back to the big sex strike. You're not exactly the Teamsters or Sanitation Workers, actress ladies. Striking works when it inconveniences your fellow citizens enough that they pressure management to cave. A Personal Sex Strike is even stupider than if boiler-room phone solicitors struck (please, God) or the IRS Audit Division decided to picket until they got higher wages. See, those examples would be work stoppages that every sane person would be hoping would go on forever. Similarly, no one on earth cares whether any of you ever have sex again.

Some questions to the mighty strikers and their spokes-twits:

Whom, exactly, do you believe the withdrawal of your sexual favors will affect? Do you honestly believe that the lawmakers in Georgia or Alabama are going to learn that you plan not to have sex and say, "Well, dadgum it, I'm convinced! Terminate all the pregnancies you want as late as you want, if it means that I can sleep again at night knowing that your third husbands, tennis instructors, casting directors, co-stars, or pool boys will no longer be denied the pleasure of your company!"

You've already made perfectly clear that your interest in sex is not to make babies. Okay, fair enough. Mine either, anymore. And if you are willing to use sex as a bargaining chip, you must not consider it one of the great joys of life. You obviously think of sex not as a way to express love or even just to have a good time, but as a weapon to wield as suits you. An angry feminist acquaintance used to call that "applying the vaginal wrench." It works equally well to get parts in movies or to punish men. With that attitude, who will miss it if it is withdrawn? My guess is that some of your husbands won't even notice the difference.

And finally, Irony is completely lost on these women. Ladies! Your form of protest is also a definitive way to eliminate the need for abortion! Can you imagine the gnashing of teeth, the rending of garments, the profanity-laced rants, if Pro-Life people suggested that one way to avoid getting pregnant is to refrain from having sex? Oh my. One of so many things you can't say aloud without calling down the Wrath of Hades in a Twitter Storm.

Be that as it may, one way to HAVE sex and yet avoid abortion is to confine yourself to birth control PLUS protected sex and then only with men who would be husband and father material instead of soul-deadening drunken hookups. Then, in the unlikely event that the condom broke AND your birth control failed simultaneously, the man involved would not be someone you just met at a party whose last name you don't know. He could even be eager to be a husband and father! Ah, I know – crazy talk. I blush to state such old-fashioned ideas.

Last week, John Hinderaker discussed exhibitionist young activist/model Emily Rat-something, disrobing (again) to protest stricter abortion laws in a couple of states. (Funny, isn't it, how "sanctuary" only works one way…) Now, in previous naked protests, the blimps of Code Pink (which should be renamed "EYE BLEACH – STAT") have protested stuff they disapprove of — like Supreme Court nominees or fighting back against terrorism — by lumbering around in the altogether brandishing signs. Sadly, this has not caused pacifism so much as a measurable uptick in commitment to either homosexuality or celibacy by any men unlucky enough to have caught sight of them.

This was not the case with Miss Emily, which is why I suspect Mr. Hinderaker, with his unblemished track record of appreciation for feminine beauty, featured her. If I looked like that, I might never wear clothes again. But, seriously, what the heck? A beautiful young thing getting naked would not automatically spring to mind as a tool for promoting a sex strike.

So I'm going to speculate that she just likes to be naked and especially likes to be looked at appreciatively. Fine. Miss Emily, you don't need to invent a reason to do that. Just spare us the accompanying incoherent drivel. Here is the gist of but one of her pearls of wisdom: "The right-wing hates abortion because it needs bodies for the prison-industrial complex."

That exactly sums up what motivated MY Mama when she had a high-risk, nearly-fatal pregnancy with me and refused a medically-advised “termination.” How I avoided prison is anyone’s guess. My mother would not consent to what legitimately fell under that vanishingly small percentage of abortions “to save the life of the mother.” She refused it and rolled the dice. They did the C-section at just over six months. In 1946, in a small rural hospital with no neonatal nothin’. She spent six weeks in hospital and I spent three months in incubator. Basically, she gave me life – twice. We were as close as a mother and daughter could be for 70 years.

However moronic the patriarchy-prison crap sounds, I also guarantee that Miss Emily did NOT think it up by all by her naked lonesome. That has to be straight out of some indigestible word salad on Intersectionality. So, Emily, please, just disrobe as the spirit moves you, and I promise if you stop with the gibberish, that I will leave my clothes ON. Well, at least in public.

THE 2020 ELECTION IS ALREADY OVER

May 31, 2019

Well, it's official, my friends. Some no-name polling outfit – Lying4DemocratsRUs? – has done a, like, totally scientific poll that showed Slow Joe Biden 5 points ahead of President Trump. In my ARIZONA!! Goodness gracious, what a harbinger of things to come if he can't even win a Deplorable-Filled, Gun-Totin' State like AZ. They are already speculating about how PDT is going to make up those lost electoral votes. Talk about premature prognostication.

Not only that, but Hillary has a 98 percent chance of winning. Oh wait. I'm sorry. THAT, like, even MORE totally scientific poll was the NIGHT BEFORE the 2016 election, not a year and a half in advance. YouTube "Election Night 2016" and watch the malevolent moronic media me-monsters chortling with glee at their rosy predictions. And then when the actual results come in, watch them crumple like the witch in The Wizard of Oz when doused with water. I try to do it at least once a week. It's better than Prozac as an anti-depressant.

It's hard to pick a favorite moment from that night. Was it smirky little Rachel confidently informing her acolytes that "even if Trump has HIS BEST NIGHT EVER" that he just had no possible path to 270 and was doomed to lose? Or was it the hyperactive little toadie with his map of all 57 of the states, pointing out that IF things went particularly badly for Bad Orange Man that he could even lose Texas, Georgia, Arizona, and South Carolina in Hillary's Historic March to the Greatest Beatdown Ever? Comedy gold, my friends, comedy gold.

One particularly hilarious point not really highlighted in that absurd Arizona poll is that Biden was the ONLY candidate that even stood a chance. Only an old hair-sniffing, handsy white male retread whose son became a billionaire while Daddy was in office has any chance to unseat the incumbent. None of the Irritating Identicrats can possibly win.

Who wants to vote for women who eat salad with combs and abuse their staff, or tannish women who clawed their way to fame and fortune the old-fashioned way by sleeping with married kingmaker politicians, or a gay mayor of an unlivable city who thinks America isn't all that great now or ever, or a semi-hysterical Spartacus impressionist?

Any of these Intersectional Slot-Fillers would be but minor footnotes in history against Trump. Kind of like George McGovern without the gravitas and military service. Plus, I think even though McGovern had some mildly silly planks in his platform, I never knew him to be anything but a sweet South Dakota guy, whereas the 2020 crop of Democrat contenders are mostly snarling, vicious, hateful snipers or rich, senile totalitarians. Or both.

This is the first prong in the Left's 3-prong strategy to undo the 2016 election disaster: keep doing fake polls that prove to regular Americans that they might as well stay home because there is no hope. It's over. America lovers: DO NOT FALL FOR THIS. In the timeless words of poet Dylan Thomas who was talking about actual death, not just the death of our Republic: "Do not go gentle into that good night; Rage, rage, against the dying of the light."

Nattering Nancy inadvertently telegraphed the second prong. When my little sister was 3 and I was 8, we were playing Hide-N-Seek in our house. When it was her turn to hide, she said, "Don't look behind the davenport because that's where

I am going to hide." Naturally, we thought that was pretty cute. As I said, she was 3.

But when Nancy prattles on and on about her bogus "fear" that Trump won't abide by the outcome of the 2020 election, she might as well have tattooed on her neck in the manner of her MS-13 homies, "WE INTEND TO CHEAT. OPENLY, PROUDLY AND MUCHLY. But, you Deplorable Racists and Trump better not question the results."

I am told that in Tucson there are currently – it probably changes by hundreds a day – 7,000 MORE illegal aliens than already resided there. Seven thousand extra "harvested" votes is a lot to overcome even in a proud Red State like my Arizona. It does little good, of course, to stash their illegals in Deep Blue states like California and New York. Since we live in a Republic with the Electoral College the losing losers pledge to abolish unless they spread out the cheating, it will do them no good if all the same electoral votes go to Trump 2020.

Every time there has been a Republican in the White House – Nixon, Reagan, Bush Sr., W, and now Trump – the Chicken Little Caucus has squawked that the Republican President will fail to vacate the premises when his term is over. There was even an SNL sketch about Nancy Reagan hanging on to doorknobs and having to be carried out of the White House like cordwood. Never mind that it's never happened. Without fail, the First Family has packed up its stuff and left with its dignity and the White House silver intact. Well, the Nixons left rather more prematurely and the Clintons grabbed as many souvenirs as they could carry. Their dignity sailed decades ago on a ship called The Blue Dress.

The third prong of the Left's brilliant election strategy is just the time-honored "chicken in every pot" promise – only this time the football-team of candidates (24 and counting…) is vying to see who can promise the most absurd number of freebies. Absolutely free college! Major in Transgender Studies and stay for 12 years! Free income for life! Work is for the suckers who will pay for you! Free birth control – what kind of Republican racists demand you pay $9.00 a month for birth control out of your own pockets?! Why, in a calendar year, you might have to do with one less tattoo! Free health care to any sick person who can stagger across any border! And you think the ER is fun now!?

One prong I bet we don't see this time around is a large number of unhinged celebrities threatening again to leave the country when Trump is reelected. If any of these egotists had an iota of self-awareness, it should have been mortifying when the Deplorable electorate saw mass celebrity defection as a bonus, not a threat, and voted accordingly.

Such a pity they are also pathological liars and stayed put.

THE WORST PARTY EVER!

June 7, 2019

My good friend, Minnesota neighbor, and frequent roadie when I was doing comedy was a Vietnam vet named Randy. He was and remains a gregarious, friendly salesman-type guy who knows hundreds of people from all walks of life. He once invited me to accompany him to a "party" at the home of a friend of his. Ned was going through a terrible divorce. The man's wife had not only left him for another man, but was also having an affair with her divorce attorney, apparently for a discount on his services. (Michael Avenatti, the Early Years?)

Poor Ned was not only miserable, but was also an accountant, a profession known far and wide for being a wacky, fun-loving bunch of party animals. Haha, I kid. Anyway, nobody else came to the party. Even Max, not yet the famous novelist he later became, was at that time just an ordinary law student and IT guy. He had to study for an exam.

So it was just the three of us. Festive! Ned set out some beer he had failed to refrigerate until a few minutes before the party. Randy tried to talk about current movies, but Ned did not like movies. Or music. Or jokes. Or travel. He was despondent and the divorce was all he wanted to talk about. Randy, himself recently divorced, tried gamely to change the subject. Finally, I tapped my watch, shot Randy a "wife-like" look widely understood by every man who has ever been married, and said, "Oh my, where did the time go? It's already 7:45. I forgot I have to get up early for a flight tomorrow to Rome for that lunch gig for the Pope…"

THAT was a bad party.

My little sister once was coerced into attending a Tupperware Party at which she also found herself the only guest. The hostess served champagne and a homemade Lemon Meringue Pie. My sister said the pie was inedible. While her hostess was setting out thousands of Tupperware items, Sis sneaked into the bathroom to discreetly flush her piece of pie down the toilet. Sadly, even after multiple flushes, the meringue still floated on top, peaceful as a cloud in the sky blue bowl. Eventually, she had to reach INTO the toilet and wrap the meringue in toilet tissue to make it go down. She spent most of the rest of the party washing her hands.

THAT was a bad party though it made a story that put ME on the floor.

But neither of these parties can possibly hold a candle to the wretchedness of the current Democrat Party. It really should be called The Know-Nothing Party, but, sadly, that name has already been taken.

The Party is bookended by a doddering gazillionaire who holds up two fingers and says, “Three,” and a vapid but comely young bartender whose major Green New Deal legislation to wipe out the U.S. economy, the energy industry, and climate-changing cows, was voted down unanimously. The stuttering old gazillionaire is also famous for saying we needed to pass a 3,000 page unread piece of crap legislation “in order to see what’s in it,” and that MS-13 – a vicious, murderous El Salvadoran gang whose numbers in this country surpass a military Division — is mostly famous for its spark of humanity.

Other Democrat Party stars – several not even running for President yet — include a portly Georgia woman who believes she “won” the governor’s seat, except for that one nagging little detail about getting fewer votes. And it also includes an entirely different portly woman who worked in television and gave debate questions in advance to Hillary Clinton.

Did we mention the Party's Presidential Candidates include several communists and socialists, some of whom honeymooned in the Stalinist Paradise even before glasnost? And one of whom is well on his way to turning New York City into the Union of Soviet Socialist Boroughs? Another Party star is super unique because he has a HUSBAND. How cool is that? So do I, but you don't see ME running for President because of it...

We can't forget the young former squeeze of the old married kingmaker in California, or the bigoted Somali bigamist from Minnesota, or the choo-choo loving hair-nuzzler whose son became a billionaire while his Daddy was in office. Unfortunately, he is an old, pale male, but he's leading the scrum of unappealing candidates. There's still time for him to come out as transgender. He wouldn't even have to change his name – just drop the "e" on Joe.

Some pundits look for a last-minute back-from-the-dead ploy by Hillary to stumble head-first into the arena. (Please, God.) Or the Democrats could try to pull Oprah or Michelle out of a (very large) hat. The Pussy Hat #MeToo Party of Hating Men of Icky Whiteness and Loving Late-Term Abortion will not go willingly with another Toxic Male Honky. I could go on about the pathetic human capital because we haven't even got to the chuckleheads in Hollywood or the Media yet. But let's save them for another day and glance briefly at the planks in the platform – planks that, with luck, they will be WALKING come the General Election.

The Democrat Party in 2019 America is the Party that hates everything about America, starting with the Constitution! It has come out four-square AGAINST the Electoral College, the right to defensible borders, both the First Amendment guaranteeing Freedom of Speech they call hate and also, of course, the Second Amendment guaranteeing the right to keep and bear arms. It is the Party of "a woman's right to choose to get rid of a baby right up to, during, and after birth, and selling its little parts for scrap."

It is the Party of removing every single qualification for anything except quotas by race, sex, or whatever is cool this week. It is the Party of a guaranteed income even if you are "unwilling" to work. It is the Party of 70 percent income taxes, wealth taxes, death taxes, and free medical care for illegals. It is an Open Borders Party that JFK, Truman, even FDR would not recognize today. It is a Party that hates cops, soldiers, and ICE.

It is, in short, the worst Party ever, which combines the organized intolerant thuggery of what is erroneously termed "the right" with the economic suicide – and equally murderous thuggery – of the Left. It must never win again.

The Republic NEEDS two vibrant, serious, sane parties full of representatives who love this country and want to see it thrive. Voters need an actual choice. The current Democrat Party is not one of them.

JUNIOR YEAR IN HELL

June 14, 2019

I have recently seen a poll in which the majority of millennials claim to want to live under socialism. Bully for them, and don't let the door hit you in the bum on the way out, kiddies. One of my favorite comedians back in the day was a (then) young man named Jake Johannsen. And one of my favorite lines of his was "I live in California now, but I grew up in Iowa. I was 21 before I realized I was...free to go." Well, guess what, guys? You are not only free to leave Iowa (even you, Dave Begley!) you are free to get the heck out of the entire country! You can leave here on the next plane and try your hand at North Korea or Venezuela. Take a rickety raft to Cuba. There must be at least one used raft lying around in Florida.

See, one of the easiest ways to tell which countries are good and which countries are the President's inelegantly but accurately expressed "s***holes" is to ask yourself "which countries have walls to protect their borders from invasion and which countries have walls to PREVENT their own people from leaving?" Many young people won't understand that difference until they desperately want to leave but find that they can't. This really couldn't be simpler. But our miseducated youth who got all their post-college news from Jon Stewart have no idea of what life under socialism is like.

I propose we organize a new public program called "Junior Year in Hell" for all these idealistic socialists. Out of mercy, we will start by assigning just the morbidly-obese drop-outs from Michelle Obama's All-Arugula School Lunch Program to North Korea.

Armed with their starry-eyed dreams plus the Collected Works of Kim Il Sung, a Dennis Rodman t-shirt in 3XL, and a manual on how to forage for and prepare grass, the plucky but delicate millennials can begin a life of service to Dear Leader. Remember, comrades, you may make no eye contact with others; only look down. That's where you might find grass, anyway, or possibly a lizard for dinner. Should they be able to avoid serving as a modern-day Donner Party for the starving Norks, they could return healthier than when they left. Assuming Orange Man Bad can get them freed.

Ah, but I hear the little spittle-flying loudmouth yet fragile darlings say, "No, no, we don't mean an icky POOR country where they only have jeans that are torn because they are OLD and RAGGEDY, not because they are cool and expensive. We mean like, you know, like in Switzerland or Sweden, or Norway or something. Whatever."

Yes, whatever, indeed.

Okay, how about Venezuela? Lots of really important celebrities and all the cool kids in the Senate lunchroom raved on and on back in the day about how wonderful Venezuela was.

If you fly to Caracas to live, may we suggest that you bring a "support animal" with you on the plane. Oh, not a dog for EMOTIONAL support. We mean a more substantial animal for PHYSICAL support. The Venezuelan people have had it up to here with Shank of Dog and Fricassee of Zoo Animals. For that reason, we suggest your Support Animal be a large steer or a flock of chickens. Don't worry about the airlines – they are, like, totally cool with Support Animals, even when somebody's Support Snake bites her seatmate. The legal system is currently geared to favor the clinically insane and corporate entities are loath to offend anyone in that protected category, which is why middle-aged men in lipstick are free to potty in the same restroom as little girls in Target.

Now one thing you should know is that when you get to Venezuela, there is an excellent chance that your Support Animal livestock will be stolen. Excuse me. “Stolen” is such an ugly and judgmental word. We mean to say “expropriated” or “confiscated” or “redistributed,” as Candidate Obama explained in a rare candid response to an innocent question from Joe the Plumber in a late campaign stop in Ohio. Whoa, doggies! Obama’s handlers were not at all happy he had gone off the “Hope and Change” message to inadvertently mention he planned to steal from the productive to give to the slackers. Color Joe surprised when minutes after his simple question, there was an anal probe into every area of his life.

Meanwhile, back in Venezuela: When your Support Animal stash is either stolen or just eaten up, you will be dependent on the Maduro government for food. No problem, just remember never to say a critical word and you, too, may get twelve daily grains of rice and 3 beans. For Heaven’s sake, do NOT wear a t-shirt that says: “Hey, Venezuela, suck it up; you guys VOTED for this!”

Socialism is really the ultimate form of greed. Oh, the big bad capitalists are always being accused of being greedy. Coming up with a world-changing idea – like Amazon or Spanx – and getting incredibly rich, paying the salaries of thousands of people is “greedy” in LeftWorld. TAKING stuff from the ones who earned it is “fair.” You betcha.

President Obama once queried aloud, “At some point shouldn’t people just say that they have enough?” We are on the same page here, Barry. The concept of “contentment” is very important to me. Our income stream and life savings are modest, but plenty. One of the ways to have "more" is to want less. Even if I won the lottery tomorrow, which seems unlikely since I don't play it, except for having fun giving it away, there's not one thing I crave or need. I wouldn't even trade in my beloved 6-year-old Hyundai Sonata.

Oh, I might want to purchase that gorgeous white and navy sheath our beautiful First Lady wore in England, if it comes in size Pudgy Munchkin, but substituting cowboy boots and a "Girls Just Wanna Have Guns" ballcap for the elegant white hat and stilettos, is just not going to have the same impact.

But, Barry, are there no mirrors in your new mega-mansion? Wikipedia says the Obamas are now worth $40 million, which I think is an underestimate by many orders of magnitude, but, good to know that they won't be digging through dumpsters for their arugula. That's quite an impressive haul for "public service." Commie Fidel had $300 million, the relatives and hangers-on of every tinpot dictator the world over — whether the late unlamented Yasser Arafat or Hugo Chavez's relatives — are richer than almost everyone but Jeff Bezos, and at least he worked for his.

SO, IT'S COME TO THIS, HAS IT?

June 21, 2019

Not to alarm dear readers or anything, but a couple of things have happened since our cohort all pretended to have been at Woodstock: namely, we got old and infirm and the world has gone completely mad around us. When did this happen? Boy, I can't count the times that I have heard that stupid saying about putting frogs in cold water and then slowly turning up the heat so that they don't jump out until it's too late. But who knew that was actually a thing? I mean, who would even boil a frog for any reason?

Oh sure, we noticed a few things. The excellent novelist Max Cossack reported to me in his early 30s that he had gone to play a game of pickup basketball at the Y with friends and he leapt up for the ball and NOTHING HAPPENED! He did not leave the ground, which surprised and dismayed him. And this was a guy who still weighed within a few pounds of what he weighed in high school and who worked out several times a week, but no Tim Duncan, he.

A t-shirt I saw recently mourned this shift amusingly: "Childhood injuries: falling off the bike, falling out of a tree; Adult injuries: sleeping wrong; sitting too long; sneezing." Pathetic. My friend, Randy, who I have written about on numerous occasions, once sneezed without bracing for it and was reduced to lying on the living room floor for over a week! He, who was once a 20-year-old combatant in LZMary in Vietnam. He, who set track records in his Sioux City, Iowa high school that were not broken for over 25 years.

I have written previously of my infamous "Sudoku Injury" in which I sat bent at an angle over the table working a 6-star level Sudoku puzzle for a couple of mindless, frustrating hours until I attempted to get up and felt a worrisome "snap" and found that I could not straighten up any further than Groucho Marx walking with his cigar. That was in my late 50s and the muscle spasm lasted for three agonizing days.

Also discussed on at least a couple of occasions has been my rotator cuff injury sustained in a losing dustup with a sliding glass door. Since that revoltin' development, I bet I have seen 20 other people roughly my age in the tell-tale slings. "Rotator cuff?" "Yup". "So sorry."

There's no telling how the Hammacher Schlemmer catalogue folks got somebody to sell them my name and address. But I used to see it once in a while in the distant past when it featured high end adult toys (no, not that kind…) for people with way too much money who need a life. Well, guess what they mostly offer now? Let me list a few items:

The Easy Read Clock; The Voice Clarifying Over Ear Amplifier; The Compression Knee Massager; The Chin and Neck Toner (with humiliating picture); The Pain Relieving Foot Tent; The Neck and Shoulder Heat Wrap; The Strongest Outdoor Rocker (can support 600 lbs. – Seriously?! For the 500 lb Grandma and her 100 lb Grandbaby?); The Under Clothing Lumbar Pain Relieving Belt; The Plantar Fascitis Orthopedic Walking Shoes; The Crow's Feet Reducing Skin Toner Wand; The Circulation Improving Hand/Wrist Massager; The Circulation Improving Leg Wraps. The LED Lip Rejuvenator, a steal at just $99.95; The Best Compression Socks. It goes on. Believe me, it goes on.

Do you see the pattern here? The target market is wealthy, old and has "issues." Some of these issues involve better living through chemistry. The Golf Channel, for example, is largely sponsored by Cialis, featuring happy couples resting comfortably post-encounter in separate waterless outdoor bathtubs for reasons best known only to themselves.

And the world around us? Most of it you couldn't even make up.

When I was a young married lass, Gillette used to sponsor Friday Night Boxing, called the Friday Night Fights. "Be all a man can be!" said their ads. I was never a boxing fan, but often, as young marrieds working all week and feeling stressed, we would get particularly cranky at each other on Friday nights and we used to joke that Gillette should sponsor our spats.

It's no secret what the chowderheads who run the company now are sponsoring. Its latest ad featured an African-American father showing his daughter, now taking enough hormones to grow facial hair and pretend to be a male, how to shave. Oh, Lord, make it stop! Make it stop!

Most men I know do not LIKE shaving every day, especially black guys and Jewish guys with curly hair that gets all ingrown and problematic. DELIBERATELY choosing to grow facial hair would be right up there – though actually nowhere even close – to deliberately deciding to have monthly periods. Fortunately for all the transitioning guys pretending to be women, that is not at all in the cards. I am told – though, in the manner of Agent Maxwell Smart, "I ASKED YOU NOT TO TELL ME THAT!" – that it is possible to fashion a reasonable facsimile of some lady bits, but making those parts mortify you by staining your nice white skirt in seventh grade English class will not be happening. That's because you aren't ever going to be an actual female. Not ever. Get used to it. You will do better to pretend to be Napoleon.

Commenter friends: If someone had asked you 10 years ago whether thousands of illegals A WEEK would cross our border, pretending to be with children, pretending to be fleeing persecution, 90 percent not showing up for the hearings to address those fraudulent claims for asylum, and every Democrat, the Chamber of Congress, the Koch Brothers, and a shocking number of Republicans would be more than fine with that – would you have believed them?

Would you have believed the Democrats would boo Israel and – why not? – God, at a California convention? Would you have believed that the Democrats would vote against the First Amendment's right to free speech? Would you have believed that in the party of JFK — who was undone when his little premature baby, Patrick, died 2 days after birth — the single most important plank in the Democrat platform would be the right to kill babies in the 9th month and beyond?

Yeah, me neither.

And now I have to lie down and rest on my Gel Topped Mattress Rejuvenator while I put on my Osteoarthritis Under Clothing Knee Brace. See you next Friday. Try not to sneeze.

NO MOUNTAIN FOR OLD LADIES – Part One of Awesome Summer Road Trip

June 28, 2019

When Dodge hits 114, it's time to get out of Dodge. I have stayed in the Dusty Little Village for several summers, as a kind of Arizona gang initiation, while Max Cossack, the prolific novelist, has gone elsewhere for a variety of reasons. So it's not like I'm not tough enough to deal with 114, it's just that I choose not to.

We love Prescott, way up in the mountains and 20 degrees cooler on average than the Dusty Little Village, but this year we formulated a new plan. Why not go on a big circuit, visiting parts of this great and beautiful land we had not seen much of before, cadging free housing with a few old and new friends? We planned to spend Fourth of July Eve with our libertarian friends John and Ramona in Bozeman, MT – the picture of the berries and whipped cream-covered red, white and blue flag cake sealed the deal. We also wanted to include a couple of weeks back in MN visiting Daddy and our son and family. And finally catch the Cowboy Hall of Fame in Oklahoma City which Mr. AG has never seen.

We preferred not to drive more than 450 miles a day, give or take, so then it became a simple math problem, making the stops and distances come out right to fit with pre-arranged dates.

Our first stop was St. George, Utah, gateway to Zion National Park. Not to be missed, we were told, and not without reason.

We checked into our hotel, and asked about things to see. Jim, the young male desk clerk said that, sadly, parts of Zion were closed due to too much flooding. The gentleman did not mention hikes or kayaking or rappelling as alternatives. No. Here is what he said exactly:

"There is a pie place in Veyo, Utah, about 15 miles from here that has the best pie in the world."

He took one look at me and the first word that came to his mind was "PIE!" And unlike the professionally offended, I was not only not upset, I was grateful. At the tiny little pie place that was strictly takeout, they had a line longer than the first day of an iPhone upgrade. After a long deliberation with people behind me in line clearing their throats like a mass allergy attack, I chose the Raspberry Rhubarb and floated to heaven. May God Bless Jim, the desk clerk, and all his relatives, living and dead.

We did, however, decide to visit something called Gunlock Falls. I suppose I was attracted, at least in part, to the name. You can Google it, of course, and see how lovely it is. A large group of people, mostly parents with young children, plus a handful of geezers like us, were peering over the edge of a steep cliff. Evidently, one had to go DOWN before one could cross a little stream and then go up another steep, rugged incline to where one could view the falls.

There was an apparently treacherous path down that had a few large rocks embedded in fine, red silt. Some athletic teenagers were scampering – but carefully – down this path without breaking a sweat. My husband decided to go back to the car for his climbing gloves. To my certain knowledge, he had used them perhaps once or twice in 20 years and they were probably in about the same shape as OJ's famous crumpled glove, only with less blood. Multi-talented Max is also a fine piano player and takes very good care of his hands.

While he was gone, I decided to surprise him and go down the trail myself. Gingerly, I took the first step and slid about 18 inches while frantically grabbing the nearest rock and hanging on for dear life. Oh. So, this fine red silt is also slippery. Good to know.

You know how those nature shows always feature gazelles being stalked by things like cheetahs and the cheetahs are smart enough not to choose the young, tender gazelles who can run fast and kick and bite? Yeah, they always look for the sick, old and infirm gazelles, the kind they can easily cull from the herd. The kind that later – in a tasteful, distant shot – they show being devoured by a pecking order of hungry predators: the original killer, then his wife, children, and good-for-nothing relatives, then smaller mammals, various bone-cleaning birds, and finally, worms. Something to look forward to.

Heck, I remember one show we watched in which a mountain goat, barely out of the womb, ran and ran and ran and ran on a thin precipice and evaded capture by a wily coyote for a very long time until the coyote just gave up and decided to go look for a gecko. Must have been terribly disappointing, like when you have Thai food on the brain and you get there and find out it's closed on Mondays and have to get pizza instead.

So Granny Ammo, the chubby arthritic mountain goat of late, late middle age, made her way down the trail, bent over and sideways, one cautious and terrified step at a time, while trying to think of a good story to tell the ER people that made more sense than what I was doing.

And eventually I reached the bottom and the little stream that needed to be forded! By this time, a stunned Mr. AG, had noticed that his scaredy-cat wife had somehow slid and crawled and grappled her way to the bottom. Color him shocked but impressed!

So now I'm at the bottom and there's nowhere to go without being Medi-Vacced out, except UP. The path was slightly less steep going up and the reward at the top promised to be great. But, first, the little stream. It was wider than it looked, and deeper as well. Kids in flip-flops seemed to be stepping from stone to stone, but the stones looked slippery and I envisioned a mighty crash and a broken hip, with a merciful drowning being the only alternative to death by humiliation. I made a snap decision to just WALK across IN the water. It came over my ankles and made my socks and jeans a handy catch-all for the fine red silt for the rest of the walk, but at least I was in one piece. As the man who jumped from the 80th floor was heard to say at each floor on the way down: "So far, so good. So far, so good."

And then UP UP UP. Many small children offered assistance to the struggling old stranger, giving me hope for the country. I reached the summit with great satisfaction, every muscle in my body shaking, and admired the beautiful falls and adjacent reservoir. The people at the top pointed out a MUCH gentler way down that went around the reservoir and back to the parking area. NOW YOU TELL ME! We walked about a mile in beautiful Utah, sun shining, gentle wind blowing, and me feeling like I had just climbed Everest. Call me Hillary.

The next day I threw out my filthy shoes. Every single thing on my body hurt, including my hair, but I was filled with an irrational exuberance. On to the next adventure.

JULY THRU SEPTEMBER

July of 2019 opens with my finally getting to make my case for the terrible unfairness of the world in having the worst luck imaginable producing a decent videotape for my career. Never mind that I retired from my career as a standup comic nearly 10 years ago, I needed to get it off my chest. Read it and weep. Or laugh. Whatever.

Then the big 6-week journey throughout the Southwest continues with a piece on Why I Love America, followed by a wonderful 3rd of July shared with patriots in Bozeman, Montana. I take a brief time-out from the journey to describe the attitude of the hate-filled Leftist Squadsters toward this great and good country, and then return to the Road Trip with a piece called "Picture Postcard Round Every Bend." It was a fabulous trip.

Returning home, we discovered things to go into my every-once-in-awhile compilation called "Nuggets of Joy" wherein we strive to remember just how lucky we are even with challenges and things that don't go our way. Nature cooperated with me by providing an adorable little hummingbird nest and, eventually, two teeny tiny babies.

Then, by the end of August, there are two companion pieces discussing the state of the feminist movement and some hard truths about the scurrilous fall-back charge of "Raaacism" to everything and anything.

I gave a shot at a parody advice column called "Ask Ammo Grrrll" that readers seemed to enjoy. Then I had to bid a sad goodbye to Walmart when they caved to the gun grabbers in their decision to discontinue selling ammo. A self-defense weapon isn't much good if one can't find the stuff that makes it go bang.

Finally, we round out September and the Second Quarter with a last-gasp attack on Supreme Court Justice Kavanaugh, this one the most laughable and preposterous of all. Thanks for reading this far.

DEMO TAPE TRAGEDY – A TRAIN WRECK IN SEVERAL CHAPTERS

July 5, 2019

As regular readers know, the novelist Max Cossack and I are on a big road trip. We are having a spectacular time. However, I am having so much fun staying "in the moment," as we are often advised to do, that my "journal" consists mostly of hundreds of impressions that have not yet coagulated into coherent columns. Soon I will be in one place for over a week. Then watch me write like the wind! The Road Trip Journal will resume next Friday. It will continue until we return to The Dusty Little Village at the end of July, possibly alternating with things of a more political bent as the spirit moves me.

Meanwhile, as a change of pace, I thought regular readers might be interested in Susan's 5-year Fruitless Quest to produce ONE decent 15-minute demo tape to get more comedy work. After we learn of one disappointment after another and screw-ups that you could not make up if you tried, let us see if we can glean some universal lessons from that level of disappointment. At a minimum, you should feel better about yourself. You're welcome.

A little history is in order first. Bear with me. In 1982, I began my comedy career at the premier 300-seat standup club in the Twin Cities called Dudley Riggs. This really almost predated VHS tape, at least as a thing you had to send to a potential client. So how did people get a look at you? Are you sitting down? By GOING THERE. Yes! People came OUT to comedy clubs and observed the comedians doing their thing and laughed – or didn't – and came away thinking, "She might be a good fit for our PTA Appreciation Dinner." Next, they looked in the PHONE BOOK for your name and called you to discuss the event. Then you went there, ate a nice chicken dinner and did your act and got a check.

But, pretty soon, it was not enough for a "decision maker" to see you, like you, and hire you. Oh no. Soon, "process," which used to apply to inferior cheese, became re-purposed as a word to mean "everyone including the janitor must have 'input' into the decision." And so they needed to see a videotape.

This was bad on several levels: first, the comedian, usually on the margins of economic existence, had to produce a videotape. A four-camera shoot could cost $30,000. That was most of a year's salary for a lot of comics. Besides that, you would put your best lines on the demo tape and then everyone – including that janitor – would hear the lines and tell them to everyone who was not in the "process" pipeline and your act was more or less burned out in advance, if not stolen and sold.

But the day came when you could not get work without a tape. The HR sheeple who hired entertainment were not willing to vouch for a comedian without a large, warm, fuzzy support group signing off on it to protect their backside in case everything went south. This was not entirely unwarranted because many jerk comedians had their "clean" material on the demo tape, but after THAT 10 minutes, ran out of clean stuff and went to their NSFW stuff, causing massive post-banquet indigestion in the hiring person who was mentally updating her CV during dessert. And Political Correctness had only just started!

And so it began. The QUEST for the perfect tape. I will briefly describe only a handful of snakebit events. Since the comics I was working with at Dudley's – four young fellas in their 20s – could no way afford the $30,000, we initially tried just for an audiotape.

The young woman who ran the tech booth at the club had a massive, unrequited crush on one of the comedians. On the night of the taping, we all had terrific sets! But just as a fail-safe, we asked the girl I'll call Midge McDimwit (not her real name) to tape the second show too. Second shows were rarely as good, but again the Comedy Gods smiled upon us and that show went really well, too. Unfortunately, McDimwit had gone to the Rosemary Woods School of Taping, and somehow had managed to tape OVER the first set while not quite capturing the second set. We all sat at the comedy club's bar and, I believe through no fault of my own, I was egregiously over-served! Strike One.

Ah, but it gets so much better. A later attempt involved a fan who had access to a two-camera shoot for much less money. In an all-women's show I co-produced that ran for seven years, the six or seven women comics ponied up a small amount apiece. Though we were all nervous, happily, my set went swimmingly. At last! I had even bought a nice new dress and high heels and paid someone to do professional makeup.

Problem solved, right? Not so fast. The comic before me did musical impressions and played guitar. She had a Styrofoam wig head on which she had a Tina Turner wig. When she left the stage, she not only didn't take the head with her, she knocked it on the floor behind me. When I watched the tape – you will think I am making this up, but I am not – there was an inexplicable bewigged Styrofoam head FACE UP, on the floor behind me, right between my legs. The tape was unusable. Move over, martinis. This was a job for Pecan Pie.

I was often hired by the Minneapolis Convention Bureau to present at various conventions to bring tens of millions of dollars in business to the Twin Cities. One was in front of 3,000 National Tour Operators at a luncheon in Orlando, Florida. Just before I went on the emcee warned me that this particular crowd was notoriously chatty and inattentive. Now

I don't want to sound like a jerk here but, as we say in the business about a good show, I KILLED. The emcee told me that he had never seen this audience more into it. Yay, it was being taped! Victory at last. Haha. You know better by now, right? The stationary camera shot was fine, but the cameraman did not mic the audience. Because the laughs lasted so long, it looks like I am just standing there like an idiot in dead silence, telling joke after laughless joke.

I will just cut to the chase with the last two attempts – in a turn on VH-1's Standup Spotlight with Rosie O'Donnell, some technical glitch made them have to start the tape all over again. YOU try telling 3 or 4 jokes and then two minutes later repeat them to the same audience and see how well that goes.

Finally, a friend who worked at a local Tech School told me their Broadcasting Production Class was looking for someone to tape in four different venues as a class final project. All four sets went extremely well. Can you say "amateur"? It looked like it was shot in my mother's basement. Horrible sound. Horrible lighting. Unusable.

So what lessons, if any, can we draw from this sad saga, which is not anywhere near the complete story? I have four: One, sometimes when something is so clearly jinxed, it might be better for your mental health to just give up early. My friend Tony doesn't believe in "serendipity." Is it possible that if I had had a decent tape that I would now be so rich and famous that I was divorced, drug-addicted, or worst of all, like about 99.9 percent of Hollywood, simply an insufferable leftist lunatic, tweeting endless semi-literate obscenities at President Trump?

Two, eventually I got sufficiently well-known in the Twin Cities and a few pockets nationally that the tape was unnecessary. When a potential client insisted, I just said, "No" and hung up. The power of walking away from negotiations is such that lo, sometimes the less you appear to want something, the more they want you! And the more they pay you. Word.

Three, about the time that the PC nonsense was getting so thick on the ground that it became extremely unpleasant to work, I retired. Near the end, even a tape was not good enough. Some potential clients wanted to see your entire act in advance. Written down and reviewed by a committee! Uh, no; not gonna happen. And, also, HELL NO. I worked very clean, but it was totally offensive to be treated like a performer in the Soviet Union. Time to go.

Four, in the perfect little window of time that I performed, comedy was very good to me. Living modestly, happily, and well, is truly the best revenge. And you never know what is right around the bend — like this column!

F. Scott Fitzgerald claimed there were "no second acts in American life." But F. was wrong. What do you expect from someone with such a pretentious name? Call me S. Marie Vass. Or just A. Grrrll.

GOD, I LOVE AMERICANS!

July 12, 2019

Preview: Next Friday I will discuss the origin of this Road Trip and my fabulous Third of July time at the Baden Ranch in Bozeman, Montana. But today I offer these observations:

The natural beauty of this great and good country can scarcely be overstated. A trip through the Southwest, West and Midwest which starts out from the desert and canyons of Arizona and includes Zion National Park, Shoshone Falls in Idaho, the mountains and rivers of Oregon, the Columbia River in Washington, the Badlands of North Dakota, virtually all of Montana, plus the lake country of Minnesota will knock the socks off anyone who is paying attention. But ultimately a country is more than just geography, no matter how beautiful. I'd like to tip my hat to the American people.

First of all, peace be upon the late, great Karen Carpenter, I am pleased to report that America has definitely solved its anorexia problem. After three weeks of eating sinfully good restaurant food and road food from convenience stores, I can report that I have also done my part in that national achievement. Oh my.

Okay. I'll just stipulate that several of my fellow Americans and I are fat. As I write this, I am in the Rough Riders Hotel in Medora, North Dakota, having just visited Teddy Roosevelt's really cool, rustic little cabin and the Ice Cream/Fudge Shoppe conveniently located within lumbering distance.

Max Cossack, prolific novelist and history fanatic, has informed me that Teddy Roosevelt stood only about 5'9" and, as a youth, barely tipped the scales at 123. He used to do all manner of physical exercise and power eating to try to get heavier. Alas, that happened in good time anyway, and by the end of his life, he was at or about 300 lbs., nearly two more Teddys' worth of bulk. See? Some very good and great people are fat. And we haven't even yet mentioned Winston Churchill, Kate Smith or Orson Welles.To borrow the gist of the gay liberation chant of "We're here; we're queer, get used to it," let me state: "We're fat; take that; get used to it." But we Americans have many many other fine attributes.

Americans are a people on the move. It is high season in this charming tourist area and the streets are filled with happy, smiling people who have journeyed to North Dakota from many states. License plates just in our one hotel parking lot come from Minnesota, Nebraska, Missouri, Texas, California, Washington, Oregon, Montana and, surprise! Arizona, in addition to many from North Dakota itself. Judging by bumper stickers, crosses as jewelry, and vast numbers of small unaborted children, often four or five to a family, it was definitely a Basket of Deplorables.

We are a proud people and a grateful people. On a modest plaque a couple hundred feet from our hotel are the names of six toxic male men who volunteered in 2011 to design and build the old-fashioned redwood slats to make up a fine-looking boardwalk. Further on, there is a small monument to Medora's war dead. If the Democrats ever get in again, the whole town will have to be burned and the earth salted to remove the stain of a Republican President who belonged to a band of fighters called The Rough Riders. I'm so triggered by that name, that I believe I may need another piece of Amaretto Fudge. Thank God every room in this excellent hotel comes complete with a Safe Space plush toy – in fact, a Teddy Bear tricked out in Teddy Roosevelt garb. TR was, in fact, the first "Teddy" bear!

My fellow Tourist-Americans are clearly proud of their country. T-shirts and hats bearing the reprehensible American flag abound, especially on this long 4th of July weekend. They are proud of their states of origin, their colleges, the branch of the military in which they served, and various achievements. I saw a faded t-shirt on a well-toned lad that said "Everest Base Camp – Nepal." That is definitely more impressive than "Camped Outside Fudge Shop waiting for it to open." Hypothetically.

Americans are a happy people. Sure, people on vacation are generally in a pretty good mood. But I think it goes much deeper than that. Free people are happy people. You really do have to have some kind of a screw loose to be part of the Permanently-Enraged America-Haters.

Americans are a friendly people. Before I visited Paris for the one and only time, a friend told me he had recently listened to an NPR tutorial on how Americans can get along better in France. He shared with me that the French think that Americans are way too smiley, and they do not trust that our smiles are sincere. I am a naturally smiley person. In Paris, I tried my darnedest to avoid smiling. Perhaps my waiters were a scosh less surly, hard to tell.

But here in Medora, people are friendly, saying "Good Morning" to total strangers on the street. They are pleased as punch to exchange pleasantries in line at the Ice Cream Shop, or waiting to get into a museum. We ask each other where we are from and how we happened to be here at this moment; we find out the best places to eat and what to avoid. Friendly.

Americans who have tried even half-heartedly to live by Susan's Five Rules are modestly prosperous. (The Critical 5: Stay in school and pay attention; get a job and work hard;

don't be a criminal; don't abuse drugs or alcohol; don't have babies without being married. Do these things and you may not be "rich," but you will not be poor.) Almost every tourist area in the world has jacked-up prices for food, lodging, and trinkets. Responsible people have planned for this, have saved up for their vacation, and are in jovial and expansive moods. Maybe there will be some credit card bills that will take a few months to pay off, but your average American can afford the occasional splurge to make a family memory. Especially in the robust Trump economy.

Those are a few of the things that my fellow Americans ARE. Here is what they are not: racist, sexist, homophobic, or hateful. And neither is our President. It was hard for me growing up to get my mind around the Stalinist/Fascist notion of The Big Lie: a calumny that, if repeated enough times in enough venues people would believe. But now I get it. If 9 out of 10 "news" organizations, Hollywood, has-been celebrities, Academia, the "arts," and many cowardly but powerful corporations all tell us we are Deplorable Racist Haters, a certain percentage of people will believe it.

They don't know Americans at all. That's how they got Trump. And will again in 2020.

A THIRD OF JULY FOR THE AGES

July 19, 2019

Well, friends, I warned you this Trip Journal would skip around a bit. Didn't want to be too linear or logical, which I recently learned was racist. We will talk – eventually — about the Third of July. But first, what, you may ask, makes a person just pick up and leave home, living out of a suitcase, for several weeks at a time? Motives vary.

In 2005, Mr. AG and I made a legendary three-week trip for spite. Yes, spite. We felt that the landlord of the condo we had been renting in Palm Springs was gouging overmuch for half a month. Instead of paying the asking price for the last two weeks in December, we would just travel the great state of Texas, plus such "budget" areas (haha) as Newport Beach and La Jolla. We spent roughly twice what we would have spent for the condo, but we showed HIM! Moronic financial decision notwithstanding, we had a grand time from Ft. Worth to South Padre Island to Del Rio, from Galveston to Corpus Christi to Ft. Davis, and on to California.

In 2014, I wrote several columns about a wonderful road trip with my two high school besties, Bonnie and Heather Beresford, to our 50th High School reunion. We had a rollicking good time on that journey, laughing ourselves silly, storing up memories, which now help sustain Bonnie and me since we lost our beloved Heather this spring. No one can possibly predict what amazing chain of events will follow a simple trip, but in that case, the chain led directly to brand-new marriages for two of the three travelers! Holy Cow! I have also mentioned in the past that Mr. AG read and became inspired by William Shatner's autobiography entitled *Just Say Yes* and decided that Shatner's attitude should inform our life going forward.

So one day a Happy Warrior of a Libertarian writer and scholar, John Baden of Gallatin Gateway, Montana (near Bozeman), called and asked if I would be interested in being the guest speaker for his annual 4th of July Eve celebration. Perhaps to seal the deal, he told me, "In past years, we have had seven Nobel Prize winners as speakers."

Significant pause on my part. And finally, "Uh, John, you DO know – right? – that I am a retired comic and target-shooting Arizona housewife of late late middle age who took 18 years to earn a Bachelor's Degree. In Speech." He claimed to be a big fan of the column and unconcerned about my puny academic achievements. He also let drop that he had bought over 50 of my books to give away "like Gideon Bibles." Max and I Just Said Yes!

On a yearly basis we are incentivized to get the heck out of the Dusty Little Village for several weeks in the summer. We took July 2nd as our target date to arrive at John's ranch and then planned the whole rest of the trip around that. We left June 20th which was about as much of AZ summer as we cared to experience after a mercifully cool May.

We arrived at the beautiful Baden ranch, having traveled the last 100 miles in intermittent squalls of rain, which persisted on and off for the entire four days we spent in Montana. But the showers alternated with beautiful sweet air, endless blue sky, brilliant sunshine and friendly sunny people, so it was all good. John and his lovely and brilliant wife, Ramona (to whom John refers as his "lifetime achievement award"), were amazing hosts.

First came a tour of the huge rambling ranch house. John built the core area himself from logs he cut himself, you know, like we all did. Haha. Danged impressive! Numerous areas were added as time went by, including a workout room, library, and a variety of sitting areas.

The day of the party dawned sunny and bright and I predicted that it would stay that way. Luckily, I didn't "bet the ranch." The native Montanans chuckled, looked at the cloud bank and predicted with stunning accuracy that the showers would arrive about 4:00 o'clock, right as the party was getting started. John said that was two years in a row that American Independence was celebrated in the rain. True, it wasn't Valley Forge, but it was definitely damp.

No worries. John had previously built a beautiful covered pavilion with attractive wooden tables and benches. Several helper-ladies (hey, Shauna, and Nicoletta) had set up the banquet tables for the delicious catered food: a variety of side dishes, barbecued chicken and beef ribs. Brian, the all-around handyman/sound guy (and trained helicopter mechanic, and gunsmith, because why not?) put up tall outdoor heaters that worked very well. It was a funny experience to have my "audience" standing clustered around each one. I should have SAT while the audience stood as a humorous change of pace…

By some miracle, the sound system also worked perfectly! I would guess that in my long career as a standup, the sound system was decent perhaps 70 percent of the time. Early on in my career I did a show standing in high heels on a folding chair with a Mr. Microphone.

John delivered lovely remarks about the benefits of what he calls his "Trinity" – "responsible liberty, sustainable ecology, and modest prosperity" – and then I did a wee bit of standup and read a couple of my columns that represented John's talking points. Then a misty-eyed John played an NPR professional reading of the Declaration of Independence. A very moving event. John wasn't the only one with misty eyes. It was a delight to be among patriots, even including some old-school liberals.

And then we talked, ate, laughed, ate, and bellied up to the groaning board of the dessert table. Guests had brought all manner of awesome desserts, but the absolute highlight was Miss Edie's Chocolate and Strawberry Cake decorated with the Capitol Building. It was a work of art. It was so fetching that it was all gone by the time Max got there and he had no choice but to settle for four other desserts. Sad.

One inspiring and encouraging takeaway from three days with the Badens was seeing two people a stone's throw from 80 still totally engaged with life — cheerful, optimistic, active and madly in love. John should definitely get some regular stipend from the Bozeman Visitors' Bureau. From the day he invited me to the hour we left, he bombarded me with dozens of photos of the ranch and surrounding area. He loves everything Bozeman, indeed everything Montana. I have never met a happier person. He took me to his supermarket and introduced me to his favorite carryout boy, Hans. He is also a fine cook and deadeye shot with a pistol at over 25 yards. Your Ammo Grrrll was no match for him at that distance.

Unless some political disaster intervenes demanding my shrewd analysis, it's on to the next bend in the journey. What a country! Are we blessed, or what?

YOU ARE HORRIBLE – Whatever Makes You Think I Don't Love You?

July 26, 2019

The Squawking Squad of Squealing Squirts wants us to know that America is a terrible evil place that is probably irredeemable. It may have a slim chance if we empty out all of Central America and swap those folks for our white Trump voters plus the conservatives of any color. (Which, parenthetically, would quickly turn Central America into a safe, prosperous, economic powerhouse within a few years…but that's for another day.)

Then we must put people in charge of America who couldn't run a Sno-Cone concession on the beach in August, let alone a country. (Pick any Democrat currently running…)

The Squawking Squad are of the "Hue" School of Thought made famous during the Vietnam War when some spokesman for the war actually said, "We had to destroy Hue in order to save it." Only by utterly destroying every single institution, every scrap of history, the vibrant Trump economy, the precious rule of law, the Bill of Rights, the Constitution, and every last border can America save itself according to the Squawking Squad.

But God forbid any sane person should conclude that that means they kinda sorta hate America. Out come the vicious epithets that they believe end the argument: Racist! Sexist! Deplorable xenophobe! Poopy-pants! Censure! Hair on Fire! Sky Falling!

Imagine, if you will, this tedious behavior passing muster in a relationship. Pretend someone's husband, or brother, or possibly both, says the following to his spouse:

"From the day you were born, you were hateful, racist, sexist, and supremacist. I have no idea why I ever thought being in a relationship with you was a good idea! There was never a time in your life when you were not full of hate and privilege. Nothing you do can ever make you a better person or redeem you, including voting in an unqualified black man. Twice. Sure, you have taken me into your home and fed me and educated me for free and paid for my health care but if you think that means you aren't terrible, well, you have another think coming! Oh, and by the way, under no circumstances should you suggest that I should exercise my right to LEAVE you just because I tell you hourly how much I hate you. Saying that I am perfectly free to leave you is racist, sexist, etc. (see tedious list above). Staying with you and claiming I love what you COULD be shows just how tolerant and wonderful I am."

How would THAT fly in a relationship?

From the time I heard the ridiculous phrase "of color," I understood at once what that was about. Pretending that the history of black people in this country bore even the slightest resemblance to the situation of a recent illegal immigrant from El Salvador or a recent legal immigrant from Africa in order to enlarge the Grievance Pool was as fundamentally dishonest as it gets. Like a poor naive soul, I thought, "Well, this will never work," but, of course, it did. We don't get to VOTE on what the Grievance Mongers are going to call themselves in order to enlarge their base.

It goes without saying that a dark brown East Indian spelling bee champ, Jews from the Ukraine, Chinese people who cheat in school by studying, and the pale children of coal miners in Appalachia are, by definition "without color" and have no part in the "of color" spoils.

Two members of the Squirrely Squad do, indeed, appear to be "of color." But what the hell "color" is AOC that she can yell "racism" at anyone else? I defy her to put her scrawny little arm next to my black-haired, brown-eyed Irish cousin's or my husband's Hungarian Jewish uncle's and see whose "color" is darker. Okay, "Sandy" — which is what she was called at the bar — may have Puerto Rican ancestry, but that doesn't change her COLOR any more than leopards can change their spots. Her color is beige at best. I guarantee she has never once been discriminated against in her entire life for being beige. My Afro-Honduran foster son used to favor a brand of clothing with the motto: "Love sees no color." But that was then. Now, color is ALL we're supposed to notice. That clothing would now be banned as racist.

The next person who tells me that something I think or say is "racist" I intend to answer with one word: "Good." It will mean I must have something right. Because "raaacist" is the only thing that mental midgets can think of to hurl when rational argument has failed them. It has zero ability to affect me any more. If everything is racist, then nothing is.

You want to enforce a Day Without White People on campus? Think about that for a minute and realize how far the left has degenerated from the heady days of integration. Not even to mention Free Speech.

Fine. A Day Without White People – bring it. Then, let's also have a day when nobody who is NOT white can use anything white people brought to the party – no electricity, no penicillin, no polio vaccine, no landline OR cell phone, no computers, no sewing machines, no automobiles, no air travel, no Bill of Rights, no printing press, no steam engine, no cotton gin, no radio, no movies, no television. Oh, and you can't go to Disneyland either. That, of course, does not even begin to scratch the surface. But students wouldn't know that – we don't have a White History Year or a Jewish History Month or a Cis-Normative Male Contribution Decade, do we?

On that day, when no non-whites can use any of our contributions, the Scurrilous Squad can sit in the dark without Twitter – or a phone or computer or heat or air conditioning — and think about how terrible their lives are in this blessed land. That seems to be what they do best.

A PICTURE POSTCARD 'ROUND EVERY BEND

August 2, 2019

What a country! Really. It is so beautiful, if anyone just opened his or her eyes and took it all in, he or she would be ashamed to be so enraged all the time. There is, as I've titled this column, a picture postcard round every bend. (Including, but not limited to, Bend, Oregon. Picture below of two random tourists of late, late middle age by a pretty river.) So far, I have not been in a single place, large or small, that I would not think it would be fun to live for at least a year. Or until the snow comes. Been there; done that.

Our Awesome Road Trip took us through parts of Utah, Idaho, Oregon, Washington, and Montana, which we estimated to be about 2500 miles across. Our GPS disagreed, but what does it know? Montana is yuge! And every mile so beautiful that one is in grave danger of leaving the road from ogling the scenery. Especially at their "common sense" speed limit of 80 mph. "Oh, Beautiful, for spacious skies" had to be written with Montana in mind. Sure, it's strange that there's a state law that every town has to start with "B" – Bozeman, Billings, Butte, Big Sky – but what a fabulous place! As I discussed a few weeks ago, we then moseyed on to Medora, North Dakota. People often mosey there.

Well, friends, sometimes the WHOLE DANG WORLD does a Vulcan Mind Meld and steals your idea. More than 2 months ago, long before the President's Twitter Storm du Jour – which was IDENTICAL in unspeakable horror to the Holocaust AND Pearl Harbor and slavery and A Bad Hair Day put together! – I banged out a future column. And I called it "America: Love It Or Leave It," hoping to address the 60's bumper sticker that expressed that sentiment to the scruffy protesters of the era, the vast majority of them as white as typing paper.

Being one of the pale unkempt horde invited to leave at that time, we clucked our teeth and bemoaned the fact that these peasants were so ignorant that they totally failed to appreciate that we were only trying to IMPROVE America and, by extension, improve THEM as well. Oh, there is no human more arrogant than a "woke" 19-year-old – except that same man or woman 50 years later who never grew up, never learned a thing. (And still has the same ponytail, now in grey and far far back on his bald empty head…)

Can anyone think of a single government program of social engineering for the "good" of people that ever worked out? If you had put 100 Klansmen in a big conference room and asked them to come up with something that would have been WORSE for black families than welfare, they would have scratched their pointy-sheeted heads and been unable to do it. To go from single digit unwed motherhood to 75-80 percent of (the non-aborted) black children being born to fatherless families has been a disaster of incalculable proportions for the black community and society in general. While a certain percentage of angry women may think they "need a man like a fish needs a bicycle," their unfortunate children DEFINITELY need a man to put a steady hand on the back bumper of the Bicycle of Life.

What, truly, is wrong with the message of "America: Love it or Leave It"? I believe it is quite different from "Go back where you came from," which is what the late and unlamented anti-Semitic hag Helen Thomas said to the Jews of Israel, and which the usual lying scum SAID the President told the Fraud Squad when he clearly said, "Go back and fix things there and then come and school the rest of us on how it's done."

But if this is such a revolting place, why NOT get the heck out? America is so racist that, inexplicably, we need to erect a wall to keep people OUT, including many black and brown people who are risking their lives to get IN to this racist hell-hole, but somehow the homegrown race hustlers never pick up and leave for greener (or blacker) pastures.

Why is that? There is an entire continent filled with almost nothing but people various shades of non-whiteness. Haiti, Jamaica, Barbados, DR are just sitting there crammed with people with not a speck of icky pallor. Go, already, with our blessings and be happy. Don't let us force you to remain in this concentration camp of a racist country.

Not to pick on people of color, though I am danged tired of birdbrains like Van Jones and Don Le Moan calling me disgusting names and blaming me for others' poor life decisions. But let us spare a few criticisms for the lazy, entitled, often-pudgy white radicals livin' on Mom Street and longing for socialism as they wear their stupid masks and weaponize the few milkshakes they have failed to consume. Once again, socialist paradises already exist: China, Vietnam,

North Korea, Venezuela, or the allegedly more benign versions in Scandinavia. Your Heaven on Earth is waiting for the price of a one-way ticket! Go, Bernie, and take Elizabeth and the Squawking Squad of Bloviating, Anti-White Bigots with you.

But NOBODY ever goes. Not the race hustlers, angry feminists, ancient curmudgeonly Caucasian commies, or gaggle of has-been celebrities who are always threatening to leave when we uncelebrated nobodies have failed them. Why don't they just go, already? Because they are lying through their teeth and they know it.

Where in Africa are you going to be obscenely paid for making up news and coining a moronic turn of phrase like "The 2016 election was a 'whitelash'"? There are no job openings for a Diversity Drone in Uganda or Chad any more than there's a Diversity Director of the NBA! Who in Venezuela or Norway would care what Cher or Rob Reiner or Bette Midler Tweeted? (Not that anybody cares here.)

Nope, leaving is not an option. Best just to stay put and try to destroy everything good. Occasionally take time out to harass some poor schlub wearing a hat you don't like or stick your grubby hands in somebody's salad. It's not much of a life, but it is a living.

Speaking of moving on, we also spent two weeks in Minnesota. After visiting my Papa one night, I saw a big tricked-out Silverado with the American flag and a Trump 2020 banner snapping in the wind. It made me very happy.

I saw no Prius with a "24 Democrats 2020" banner and a Hammer and Sickle flag saying, "America Sucks! Open Borders! Free Everything For Illegals; Taxpayers Will Pay your Student Loans; Reparations for Everyone Who Isn't YOU;

No Private Health Insurance; and Full-term Abortion for All, especially men pretending to be women!"

There's a hill to die on.

MORE NUGGETS OF JOY

August 9, 2019

Who can measure the collective depression, grief, and anxiety when in the space of a couple of weeks, three psychotic losers murder and maim dozens of our fellow humans? And when the Democrat/Media Megaphone bellows with one loud coordinated voice, that – despite one of the losers being a Bernie/Warren and Fraud Squad fan – it's just all completely President Trump's fault. Never was a mass murder before he was President. Well, not counting those "people who did some things." And don't mention 51 shot in Chicago last weekend.

And so when the world is too much with us, it's time to take another of my patented "Nuggets of Joy" breaks. I promise we will return to our regularly-scheduled hellish news next week. The Leftists aren't going anywhere. And with 330 million people here, if only 1 percent are mentally deranged, that's still 3.3 million lunatics who can go off the rails at any time.

For today's column, let's channel the first couple lines of the Zac Brown/Jimmy Buffett song, "Knee Deep":

> *Gonna put the world away for a minute*
> *Pretend I don't live in it*
> *Sunshine gonna wash my blues away.*

Though there is abundant sunshine in Arizona, sadly, not all of us can be "knee deep" in the water somewhere. Some of us live in a desert, which nevertheless did not keep the imaginative street-namers in our Gated Geezerland from naming the next street over "Ocean Breeze." Due to the presence of the remnants of John Wayne's quarter-million head herd, we locals have another name for that breeze, in which one can still be "knee deep."

We recently had a front-row seat to a joyous little nature drama that went on for over a month. A mama hummingbird had built an amazing little tiny nest woven into a string of lights on our front patio, about two feet directly in front of our library window. With a front-row piano bench seat for the drama.

My neighbors in Gated Geezerland seem to compete to see who can produce the most spectacular display of outdoor Christmas lights and decorations. We are Jewish, and do not participate, though I enjoy the displays. One year I bought one festive little single string of multi-colored, non-Christmasy lights in the shape of chili peppers for the front patio just for fun. After a few years, some lights burned out, but it seemed like a lot of trouble to take them down. And thus, the string became a platform for a nest.

How in the world Mama Hummingbird "chose" that space is anybody's guess. Woven into the nest there appeared to be some longish hairs that some would mistakenly call "grey" and others refer to more accurately as "platinum blonde." I shed like a Siberian Husky, so it's nice to have some of those hairs recycled.

Mama Hummingbird sat on the eggs in the nest for about two weeks, leaving every 15 minutes or so to find sustenance for herself. I understand the impetus to eat every 15 minutes, plus I am small and flighty. I am having my DNA tested to see if I am 1/32nd hummingbird. Gotta be worth a professorship at Harvard, at minimum.

We researched hummingbirds and learned a lot of interesting facts. For example, they cannot walk. They can only hover, perch, and fly. At night they go into a state of "torpor" in which their vitals drop to ridiculous levels so that they no longer need to feed themselves every few minutes in order to live. I bet I do a version of that which accounts for my miserable metabolism. If I were a car, I could drive coast to coast on one gallon of gas.

At some point, it became clear that the eggs had hatched and that there were two tiny baby birds sharing space in a nest the size of a double-wide thimble. Mama H then had to go off and find food for all three of them and return to feed the little parasites who mostly sat around with their tiny beaks in the air waiting to be fed.

Unlike with baby humans who can take up to 25, 30 years to leave the nest – if you're lucky – these little babies turned into fat, antsy teenagers in a little over two weeks! Then the bravest one flew off about a week after that. At first his brother (I went ahead and assumed their genders) appeared happy to see him gone and took over the whole nest plus his stereo. But the next day the first bird returned and schooled his brother on how it was done and encouraged him by pecking at his behind and then they were both gone! Mama H returned from a food foray, looked around for the kids, seemed to shrug and say, "Whatever. My work here is done!" and took off herself never to be seen again.

Both the Paranoid Texan (PT) and Mr. AG claim to have seen some members of the family in the neighborhood, but I have not. It was a real delight to watch that little drama unfold and a heck of a lot cheerier than hearing human birdbrains squawking "impeeeeachment," "Puuutin," or "raaaacism" tediously. But now we are empty-nesters. Literally.

Still, it was a month-long Nugget of Joy. There are others.

Sometimes God – or the PT – just gives you a nugget of joy. We were riding in the PT's truck to get a new propane tank for our barbecue grill when we passed the elementary school on the way to Walmart. There on the sign out front were two messages: “Kindergarten Roundup Monday” and “Job Fair!” to which the PT, without missing a beat, said, “Looks like the Chinese are recruiting for their factories.” The PT is a very funny guy.

I am blessed to know a lot of funny people, not least of which is the famous novelist Max Cossack, whose novels are on sale on Amazon. Max was visibly upset by the many commenters in a recent column of mine who challenged his claim of being “the worst dancer who ever lived.” He suggests a new television show called “So, You Think You CAN’T Dance,” on which the contestants cannot TRY to deliberately dance badly — they just have to dance “normally”– if such a word could be applied to these dancers, honor bound to do their best. And THEN we’ll see who will wear the crown!

Woopsie! 15 minutes gone. Time to eat.

WE WILL BURY YOU!

August 16, 2019

As a rather anxious, high-strung little girl living in Alexandria, Minnesota in the '50s, I perceived the threat from the Communists in the Soviet Union to be very real and terrifying. Remember, this was an era in which small schoolchildren practiced drills for what to do in the event of a nuclear attack. (Answer: get under your desk, a solution which even a fourth-grader could see was going to be woefully inadequate.)

I had a little sister (still do), and we slept in bunk beds. She favored the top bunk, which I felt in good conscience was a more vulnerable spot than the bottom bunk in the event of a nuclear attack. Often, in my nocturnal worries over the latest crisis in the geopolitical situation, I would carry her down to the bottom bunk with me after she fell asleep. If hiding under a desk helped, then surely the security of the bottom bunk was an extra layer of protection.

Then one day, the vague Communist threat took a turn for the worse. In November of 1956, when I had just turned 10, a fat bald Commie with the oddly musical name of Nikita said the following on the world stage: "It doesn't depend on YOU whether or not we exist. If you don't like us, or invite us or accept our invitations. Whether you like it or not, history is on our side. WE WILL BURY YOU."

If we had known the expressions 60-plus years ago, we might have said, "This (stuff) just got real." Or, alternately, "This just got dialed up to eleven!" But that level of cleverness would have to wait for a few more decades.

Banner Headlines! Breaking News! Politicians fighting their way to the microphone to denounce it! Khrushchev just said he was going to kill us all and our puppies!

And I remember somebody in the newspaper – we wouldn't get television for two more years — saying, "Hang on! That's a mistranslation of those words. He didn't say, 'We will bury you,' he said, 'we will outlive you.'" And I found that very comforting and logical. After all, we had recently buried my maternal grandfather, but we sure didn't kill him. We outlived him, and do still. Now why do I bring this up today? Stay with me…

On the third day of our recent Awesome Road Trip we ate lunch in a jam-packed Chick-Fil-A in St. George, Utah. The place was completely full at 1:30 in the afternoon and we got the last table. The drive-through stretched for more than a dozen cars into the shopping center parking lot. It made me very happy. I love to see an enterprise with both morals and guts not just surviving, but thriving. I believe it is now the second or third most successful franchise – depending on whether you count Starbucks — in America despite being closed one day every week. The totalitarian left has tried its best to keep it out of everywhere it has the power to do so; the bigots proclaim boycotts and supporters come for miles around to patronize it.

The manager of this particular Chick-Fil-A was a sweet young African-American woman who walked around to every table, chatting, welcoming, inquiring about the food and service. A proverbial "white man" (more likely than not a Christian or even a MORMON!) told her that her friendly smile was the reason that he patronized that particular Chick-Fil-A. She thanked him and clapped him on the shoulder. He immediately dialed Gloria Allred to report a sexual assault – NOT.

The Chick-Fil-A was absolutely full of beautiful young families with lots and lots of children. Perhaps they were not Mormons, but Martians, as virtually all the children were clean, obedient and well-behaved, even the lanky teenagers, two of whom offered to bus my dirty tray when they saw I was headed that way. I expected Rod Serling to appear at any moment.

As it happened, this was around the time that has-been menopausal celebrities had announced that they were going "on a sex strike" to protest any restrictions on their sacred right to kill their own babies. Still others pledged NEVER to have babies for any reason because of Climate Change or The Patriarchy or Reasons. (I admit I don't always pay close attention to the drivel they write, Tweet, or screech, so I may have missed some well-thought-out rationale…)

And I thought about the pro-children people I've known. There was the wonderful Evangelical guy in the ammo line, with his five little stair-step boys and 4 girls. I gave him one of my 550-count boxes of .22s back when they were hard to come by so the kids could plink and you would have thought I had given him a new car. There's my Orthodox Jewish spiritual leaders, one family with 14 children, many with 8 or 10. There was the Mormon family I saw on vacation in Maui with 4 little girls in muumuus and 3 little boys in Magnum PI Hawaiian shirts. The old-timey Catholics I grew up with as a wee child had 10 kids and sat around the dining room table praying The Rosary every night as a family. Can you imagine? No violent video games, no sex-drenched television, everyone not bent over a phone, but over beads!

And Nikita's mistranslated, allegedly misconstrued turn of phrase came back to me, unbidden. I wrote it down on a Chick-Fil-A napkin and put it in my fanny pak.

"It doesn't depend on YOU whether or not we exist. If you don't like us" — and BOY, do the Leftists ever not like us and tell us so at every opportunity – "Whether you like it or not, history is on our side. WE WILL BURY YOU."

"We will bury you." Because we really are literally pro-life and so much of the opposition's world is completely self-limiting, nihilistic, sterile and anti-life in myriad ways, from abortion to the economy-killing New Green Deal. How many transsexuals with their mutilated reproductive organs are going to produce future taxpayers? How many of the screeching, pussy-hat wearing harridans who hate men will ever become mothers?

And all our side has to do – besides fight like hell to make sure the Leftists never get in power again – is just continue with relentless breeding! No need for 10 children; replacement numbers will suffice. Even secular Israelis try for three — replacement, plus one for the Holocaust. Procreation will win the day. Obama used to invoke part of Khrushchev's formula every chance he got – "history is on our side." Not so much in his case, it turned out. But it is on the side of the baby-makers rather than the baby-killers, for sure.

THE END OF FEMINISM

August 23, 2019

I don't rightly remember the first time I even heard the word "feminism." As a girl growing up in the '50s, the oldest child, I do not remember a single time that I was told I could not do something or less was expected of me because I was female. And this was with a very traditional "cis-normative" father, born in 1925. You look up "patriarchy" in the dictionary, there's his picture. And a mighty handsome one, too!

But Daddy taught me to throw a spiral, hit a baseball, bait a hook, clean a fish, mow a lawn in a diamond pattern, count change back to the customer. Anything less than an "A" in any subject, on any paper or test, was unacceptable. We were not a Participation Trophy family.

In college some young ladies were just starting to read the emerging feminist literature. Someone recommended Simone de Beauvoir's *The Second Sex*, which I found tedious and polemical and just chalked it up to her being an existentialist and, well, French. It had nothing to do with me. I was 18; the world was my oyster. And then around 1969, suddenly "women's issues" were EVERYWHERE. The more rational spokeswomen made a good case that there were legitimate grievances of a discriminatory nature that needed to be addressed.

For example, Sandra Day O'Connor finished second at Stanford Law School and the only legal job she could get was as an Assistant County Attorney in San Mateo, California when she offered to work for free and share office space with the secretary! Clearly, that was grossly unfair.

When I was a typist at Evanston IBM in 1967, I asked to take the aptitude test for what was at that time a very early stage of the computer biz. With a smirk, my boss handed me the test – mostly math and logic — to take on my lunch hour. A 75 was a passing score; I got a 97. They said I must have cheated, plus I couldn't carry the tool case the guys carried, which they claimed weighed 100 lbs. Oh well. My entire life might have been different and I like the way it turned out. But, yeah, discrimination on the basis of sex did exist, was addressed by some gutsy women pioneers, and massive societal changes ensued in pretty short order.

Here's the thing: on most of feminism's early talking points and grievances, many of which were both fair and overdue, THEY WON! In a sane world, they would have declared victory, thrown a huge party, folded up their tents and banners and gone home. But, by then "women's liberation" already claimed to speak for a large victim group and was a lucrative cottage industry. It has galled me for decades that it claims to speak for ME.

If the Betty Friedans of the world were unhappy suburban housewives with nothing much to do but be homemakers (like that's a SMALL thing…), they could now be fulfilled wage workers. We won! We won! Women can now be anything we want – firefighters, police officers, doctors, astronauts, CEOs, terrible senators, soldiers, ministers and rabbis, sports reporters, boxers, pole vaulters, pole dancers, bipolar – really anything at all.

But, in a grim determination never to take "Yes" for an answer, a different breed of feminist waddled onto the scene. Feminism had taken a vicious, vindictive and male-hating turn. Like other "civil rights" movements, it turned out to have less to do with "justice" and more to do with raw, abusive power, payback, quotas, unqualified people having set-aside slots based on their plumbing, and getting rich. Society needed to make some changes. And it did. However, we've all heard the expression "Don't throw the baby out with the bathwater." Well, don't look now, but there goes the baby…literally.

Abortion was always a divisive subject. The first time Mr. AG and I heard a friend wax poetic about what a great thing abortion would be, I almost got into a fistfight with him, except he was also a pacifist! Where's the fun in pummeling a pacifist? To a non-psychotic, the very idea of killing a baby is appalling, admit it. But by the early '70s there was a growing consensus that in the first 12 weeks, the proverbial "clump of cells" should be able to be terminated. How quickly and predictably that morphed into abortion any time for any reason, including the sex of the baby, or no reason at all. I knew one certifiable, deranged feminist who used abortion as birth control. She had had 8 abortions that I heard of before I lost track of her.

Today, after ultrasound has proven that the clump of cells looks remarkably like a baby, only 7 percent of the American people agree with third trimester abortion. SEVEN PERCENT! You could get more than 7 percent to say they have had lunch with Bigfoot and Elvis. (Bigfoot selected the steak tartare; Elvis chose the Biscuits and Gravy.) Yet seven of nine black-robed arbiters set the stage for what has become legalized infanticide.

As they say on late-night informercials: But WAIT, there's more! The old guard, who educated and litigated and lobbied for the rights and privileges women have today are driven from the movement, indeed from the public square. They have failed to get onboard with the quaint and unscientific notion that sex is a more or less imaginary construct and can change on a whim. How shocked Eve Ensler must have been to find that her tedious but lucrative play about chattering vaginas is now verboten because "some women don't have vaginas." Though she died in 1986, De Beauvoir herself wrote, "If you live long enough, you'll see that every victory turns into a defeat." Gotta love those cheery existentialists!

Newly-minted women who are actually men can now win every athletic competition against real biological women. Title IX has been rendered meaningless. Protest if you dare, even if you're an iconic lesbian tennis pro, and you will face a Twitter storm or legal action in Canada. Even backpedaling and groveling will not save you. As the famous novelist Max Cossack queried the other day over breakfast: "If men and women are exactly the same, why don't we see women who've transitioned into 'men' winning athletic events against other men? How come that only goes one way?" Bueller? Mueller? Is that in anybody's purview?

So what you might call Fairness Feminism is dead. The loony ghouls feasting on its corpse will carry on, but it will never again approach being any kind of mass movement. Normal Americans – of all colors – do not believe that a horny teenage boy who touched a breast 40 years ago is retroactively guilty of "assault." Women cannot decide decades after a drunken, consensual sexual encounter that they have been "raped." The American people do not believe that killing a full-term newborn baby has anything to do with "healthcare." Fairness resonates with normal people; lunacy does not. Normal Americans know the difference.

SOME HARD TRUTHS ABOUT "RACISM"

August 30, 2019

Last week, one of my commenters, in need of a humor fix, felt that the column was less than funny. Well, this one isn't a barrel of laughs, either. Maybe next week...

TRUTH #1: If there were a magic wand to wave to make every single white person in America erase even the slightest shadow of a penumbra of an unconscious racist thought, prejudice, or microaggression, not a single thing would change in the black communities.

Because the problem in Chicago and Baltimore, in Ferguson and St. Louis, is not that white people think ill of black people. Who cares what white people think about anything? The problem is drugs, gangs, criminal behavior including black on black crime, poor education and work skills, and fatherless children. The REAL "elephant in the room" is not white racism. It is the paucity of young black men even graduating from high school (under half in most urban areas) their lack of preparation to compete in the economic world. Add in a criminal record and a substance abuse problem, and you've pretty much screwed the pooch. Black people who do stay in school, and avoid drugs or criminal activity, are doing fine. Especially in the Trump economy.

The most intractable problem is that far too many black men act like sperm donors rather than fathers, making babies with multiple partners, babies whose mothers they have no intention whatsoever of marrying, babies who they will neither support nor raise. I don't see how they can even look themselves in the mirror every morning. It is a national disaster that has unfolded like a slow-motion car wreck that any fool could have seen coming. (And naturally, this attitude has spread to the white working-class as well.)

It has been aided and abetted by the feminists' 50-year War on Men and Boys, on, indeed, the very concept of masculinity. It is that war that is toxic, not our husbands, sons, and brothers. The anti-male bigotry sickens me to my core, as racial prejudice did from the first moment I became aware that it existed. How many lost young men, who shall deliberately remain nameless, have gone off the rails and concluded that since they were already "toxic," they might as well try to achieve at least notoriety – in El Paso, in Norway, in New Zealand, in Dayton, in Dallas?

TRUTH #2: I have said before, and I will repeat: if you had put 100 Klansman in a room and had them scratch their pointy-sheeted heads to try to think up something that would have been more harmful to black people than welfare, they would have been unable to do so.

But the Democrats got their "Great" Society which not only didn't erase poverty, but didn't even make a "Grateful" Society. It did produce a permanent, entitled, angry bloc of reliable, dependent Democrat voters. Some charge that was a feature, not a bug, but I do not think that badly of my fellow Americans, even Democrats. I believe it was another proverbial road to hell paved with good intentions. Unfortunately, once that ball got rolling, it was no easier to stop than an avalanche. Look at the pushback on President Clinton when he tried to trim the welfare rolls. Oh, the children! The children! They will be thrown into the streets! Well, no. There was a period of robust economy and people got off their behinds and worked. Just like the people who had to work to pay the taxes supporting the welfare recipients.

TRUTH #3: The VAST majority of white people have no influence whatsoever over any hiring, firing, or anything else that could affect black people. If they have Wrongthink Thoughts, it matters not a whit in the real world.

I grew up in a small town in rural Minnesota where we had not one single African-American resident. We said Negro, not “colored,” which was considered low-class. Nobody I knew ever used the “N” word. They would have been shunned. It was first said – only once – in my home by a black gangsta pal of my black Honduran foster son. The kid was shocked when I told him, “Never again. Not in my home.”

In my entire working life, I have only been a very low-level employee (usually on night shift) or a freelance entrepreneur. I have hired nobody ever, so had no opportunity to discriminate even if I were a virulent racist who desperately wanted to. I have never owned a rental property and never will. My father owned two apartments over his drugstore and the problems he had with young white women renters convinced me I wanted no part of it ever.

TRUTH #4: If racism is so pervasive, so endemic in white people’s DNA (as the half-white Lightbringer charged), then why should white people even TRY to fix something which is genetic and immutable? It is a vile lie. The overwhelming majority of white people are NOT racists, including the President.

TRUTH #5: The weaponization of nasty, slanderous epithets as a substitute for rational argument will destroy this nation. #MeToo and the embrace of the accompanying concept of “credibly accused” has already distorted and will eventually destroy jurisprudence. Screaming “racist” at everyone who disagrees with something or someone is simply calculated to shut down debate and end free speech. Academia is too far gone ever to recover. The New York Times has promised it will be chanting “racism, racism, racism” till November of

2020 — The “om” of a dying cult that desperately needs to keep black people on the Democrat plantation.

TRUTH #6: Neither can we pretend that terrible racism never existed. Slavery was a horrific institution, absolutely not unique to America. It took over 600,000 American deaths to cut out the cancer, and another century to try to cauterize the wound. No American today owned slaves and no black person has picked cotton in chains in 150 years. It is way beyond time for us all to take responsibility for our life decisions, both individually and culturally.

TRUTH #7: NO. We do NOT need any more “conversation” on race. We need to shut up and start emphasizing our commonality rather than our superficial differences — treat each other as individuals and not walking bags of melanin or lack of same. We need to pull together, love each other, and love America. If you do not love America, then find somewhere you can love, because, frankly, I am sick of listening to you. Lookin’ at you, Don “Stinky Fingers” LeMoan, Van Jones, Kneeling Colin, and every self-loathing white actress or Democrat candidate who claims to be mortified about being white. Grow up. You have so much more to be embarrassed about.

ASK AMMO GRRRLL

September 6, 2019

As a service to my loyal readers, periodically I will entertain questions. The great 12th Century rabbinic sage Maimonides wrote his famous *Guide for the Perplexed*. This, sadly, bears no earthly resemblance to that.

Dear Ammo Grrrll: Do you think regular working people who pay taxes and raise kids and volunteer and go to church and join the military and don't do drugs and don't commit crime are actually offended at being called "Deplorable," or are they just "fragile" like Spike, my Advanced Intersectional Feminist Studies teacher says?

Zelda Zinn in Oberlin

Dear Zelda: I gotta plead ignorance on this one. Why don't you ask Madame President Hillary Rodham Clinton if that had any effect on the outcome of the 2016 election?

Dear Ammo Grrrll: Is there a "faith tradition" that allows a girl to marry her brother, divorce him, eventually marry the father of her three children, then divorce him when you are off cavorting with an icky white guy married to somebody else?

Confused in Cottage Grove

Dear Confused: Evidently.

Dear Ammo Grrrll: Are there any Muslim countries where the above behavior referenced by Confused in Cottage Grove would get a woman killed?

Worried in Walnut Creek

Dear Worried: Several. But usually the government would not need to get involved. The woman's brothers would take care of it. Including the one she married.

Dear Ammo Grrrll: There are a lot of elderly, over-the-hill singers, actresses, and actors who spend all day every day Tweeting vulgarities and making totally illegal threats aimed at the duly elected President of the United States, whom I am beginning to think they don't like. What would you call them?

Grossed Out in Grosse Pointe.

Dear Grossed Out: Rob Reiner, Michael Moore, Babs Streisand, Bobby DeNiro, Bette Midler are just a few of these entertainers now in their 70s who think it's cool to act like a middle school dropout who has just discovered a whole bunch of new naughty words. I call these people "Obscene-iors."

Dear Ammo Grrrll: Sorry, Grossed Out here again with a follow-up question so popular with the vapid me-monsters in Presidential news conferences: Why are these Obscene-iors all so gosh darn fat?

Dear GO: I'm not really comfortable "weighing in" (haha) on anybody else's excess poundage, as I have had a couple of issues with this over the decades myself, but my best guess is that, contrary to popular belief, alfalfa sprouts and rice cakes are actually fattening. I recommend that every food that CAN be fried should be fried. Chicken, steak, rice, potatoes, green tomatoes, and Mexican ice cream. Fry 'em all! You will still be fat, but happy!

Dear Ammo Grrrll: Don't you feel as guilty as I do for being white?

Kristin Gilligrand-Standing in Iowa

Dear Kristin: How DARE you assume my race? If I could find my cheekbones, I have no doubt that they would be unusually high.

Dear Ammo Grrrll: Well, if you don't feel guilty for being white, do you at least acknowledge that you have only succeeded in life from your vast white privilege?

Persistent in Poughkeepsie

Dear Persistent: No.

Dear Ammo Grrrll: Say, have you read any good books lately?

Sharon Shill

Dear Ms. Shill: Why, YES I HAVE, thanks for asking! What would you say if I told you that the prolific novelist Max Cossack has his THIRD novel out and it's a hilarious satiric caper in which an obnoxious left-wing professor at a small college in Minnesota gets what's coming to him? Would you go to Amazon and click on "Max Cossack" – Simple Grifts and buy several copies to beat the Christmas rush? One stop shopping!

Remember that great scene in the movie *Witness* where Harrison Ford is hiding from corrupt cops and he is trying to blend in with his Amish protectors? He goes into town and some bullies believe that he won't fight back and push an ice cream cone onto his nose? And he says, "You're making a mistake." It's a great scene in a great movie.

Well, now imagine that this obnoxious professor has given a rural genius kid an "F" in the PC prerequisite course he absolutely needs to get into the University. But the kid won't knuckle under and regurgitate the balderdash he is supposed to repeat. The professor – like the bully in *Witness* and all bullies in academia – is making a mistake.

Watching him get his comeuppance in a complex and extremely funny "sting" – with a cast of delightful characters from Max's previous two books plus some quirky new ones – kept a permanent grin on my face throughout the whole book, except for the many times I was laughing out loud disturbing the neighbors.

Yeah, I know, he's my husband. Trust me, it's terrific. You know, certain people love to brag that they work for a "non-profit." Well, the amount of money we make from these books (all seven between the two of us) would last us for the rest of our lives, providing we die by Thanksgiving. So it's definitely not for anything as gross as PROFIT that I ask you to buy it. It's because it's really funny and you will enjoy the heck out of it, comedically and politically! I am only thinking of you, because I love you! You're welcome.

BYE BYE, WALMART, BYE BYE

September 13, 2019

Et tu, Walmart? Seriously? Do you have no idea who your customer base is?

Well, whatever. I'm done. It's a shame, too, because Walmart is the definite Big Dog shopping emporium in our Dusty Little Village. For groceries, I have two other choices in town, one of which I have always preferred anyway: Bashas. It is a pleasant, to-scale kind of local place with good meat and produce, sun screens over parking, the most customer-friendly cashiers, and slightly higher prices on canned goods. So be it. I'm willing to pay a few extra bucks for my principles. And one of my main principles is that I do not enjoy being taken advantage of without at least being treated to dinner first. (That's as gently as I can express it…) For stuff like household goods, we also have a second option called Fry's.

The hurt comes more from the betrayal than the lack of availability for more ammo. Barring the complete collapse of society and the ensuing cannibalism advocated by climatistas, I'm good for the duration ammo-wise. (As perfectly as my thighs would work into the currently popular KETO paradigm – 70% fat, 25% protein – no hungry post-apocalyptic weather wuss is going to get a crack at them as long as I have one box of .45s left.)

And though I have spent, literally, tens of thousands of dollars in Walmart, not even COUNTING the thousands of dollars on ammo alone, I understand that my contribution will not be missed. The Walton family heirs will survive with their tens of billions (with a B) intact, never once querying: "Where the heck is Ammo Grrrll? And her Visa?"

The Kneeling NFL does not miss me on Sundays and the feeling is mutual. Hollywood does not care that I do not watch their loathsome movies.

But I wish I had a dollar for every time I had defended Walmart to the liberal scolds who "would never set foot in that place." Telling them that the average working class family saves about $2500 a year on groceries and other necessities never cut any ice with them. Neither did reminding them that, especially in a place like rural Minnesota, it is very stressful shlepping two small children in snowsuits from store to store. Walmart – to a lesser extent Target – is truly one-stop shopping.

Now I guess we get to choose between enriching the CEOs who want men in the restrooms with your little girls and the CEOs who won't sell you what you need to exercise your constitutional right to defend yourself. Funny how the Golden-Parachuted crowd always drifts to soft landings behind armed guards and gated mansions. There are never real consequences for the boneheaded corporate decisions they make.

I will go to one of several local gun shops for ammo or order off the Internet. Hopefully, they will have a lot of the new Joe Biden-endorsed Barney Fife Model Magazines that hold one round only. Don Knotts, of course, used to carry his single bullet in his shirt pocket, but in a dust-up with a cartel member – lookouts for the cartels camp a couple miles from us in the Arizona hills – a single bullet will surely come in handy.

Joe Biden is quite the expert on home defense. He instructed his wife, the highly-credentialed DR. Jill Biden, in the event of an intruder, to "walk out with that double barrel shotgun and fire two blasts outside the house." Yes, indeedy, there's a plan, fully HOA-compliant.

This excellent advice of randomly firing a shotgun off your back porch — in synch with his randomly-firing synapses – was even improved upon in an interview he later gave to Field and Stream Magazine in which he recommended that one should just go ahead and fire the shotgun THROUGH the door. Now, you're out of ammo, and have killed a Jehovah's Witness and a Girl Scout selling cookies before you even got a chance to sniff her hair! Sad.

For eight years, this imbecile was a heartbeat or one arugula choking incident or stray golf ball to the head away from the Presidency. And he continues to be in first place in the hearts and minds of Democrat voters in the current primary race. That's because he's the "sane moderate" in a field so bizarre that it cannot even be parodied.

("You have an idea for an SNL sketch about the DNC primary and there's a fake Indian Totalitarian who could be the only woman in America less pleasant than Hillary; a fake Hispanic Irish man-child; a Spartacus-impressionist with an imaginary friend, T-Bone;, AND a white half-Indian woman pretending to be African-American? Plus a crazy ancient Commie who owns three homes but no comb. Come ON. Nobody would believe that…")

But back to Walmart. During the two years' long ammo drought, I stood in line there for hours and hours a day and, at one time, knew the names of some 42 employees! It cannot be a coincidence that barely a half dozen of those employees are still there. You never hear tales of how great it is to work at Walmart. My favorite cashiers at Bashas have been there since I moved here in 2010. Joline alone can make your day with just her smile and hair doodads.

I intend to deliver this "resignation" as a customer to the local Walmart management and to see that it gets to the national management as well. But I have – like my hero, Columbo –

just "one more question" before I go. Well, actually, several. Like Columbo.

• When you offend and betray your loyal customer base, do you honestly believe that the elites whose behinds you are kissing, are going to pick up the slack? Do you think any of them would deign to be sighted in a Walmart?

• Please list every mass murderer who has purchased his ammo at Walmart. Show your work. Receipts required. Just like with returns.

• Please publish the total number of rounds you have sold to normal non-criminal customers over the decades who have NOT shot anyone, ever. Feel free to round it off to the nearest trillion. Compare and contrast with the lunatics' purchases, if any.

• What are you planning to do about the ice cream-lickers who probably pose a much more serious health threat? Do you recommend commonsense tongue removal?

Maybe the current cowardly, craven CEO will resign or be fired. Maybe I will return. But not any time soon. Oh, if you only knew what a dedicated impulse buyer you are losing, famous for going in for three items and coming out with twenty-three. Ask anybody who knows me.

HORRIBLE RACIST AMERICA: FACTS ON THE GROUND

September 20, 2019

One of the strangest parts of Election Night 2016, results of which I play at least a couple of times a month when I need a lift, was the grieving, caterwauling commentariat yapping on and on about the "fear" that "everyone they know" was feeling. I have mentioned many times that I do not regularly watch television at all, let alone the pretend news programs, so I did not know one talking head from another. Disappointment, I understood, from 2008 and 2012. Mild anxiety, okay. But FEAR!? And especially among the Professionally-Diverse.

I was only vaguely aware of some of the Droning Diversity Hires. One black woman gave the questions to Hillary in advance of the debate and then dumped every diversity card in her purse out on the table in a huff: "I am a black Christian woman…" No matter. She did it. All those cards couldn't save her, but she just moved on to her next well-paid gig.

There was a humorless homophobe and general bigot with the wildly inappropriate name of Joy. There was Professional Hispanic "Republican" Ana Navarro, hatin' on Trump and predicting that it would be "sweet sweet justice" when Mexican voters would put the final nail in Trump's coffin. Oopsie! Hate must be fattening because this fake Republican seems to be getting puffier by the week. Have another churro, honey, and calm down.

At that point, mercifully, I had never heard of "credibly accused" Don "Stinky Fingers" LeMoan. But they all talked about FEAR FEAR FEAR. It was surreal. Afraid of WHAT? Not one single Hillary cough-fest or BLM or Antifa riot had ever been interrupted by icky white people. No white people stood at polling places with clubs as the unprosecuted Black Panthers had done in 2008. So what in blue blazes were they talking about?

I did recognize out and proud commie Van Jones from the little clip where Valerie Jarrett had singled him out in a crowd for reflected glory from Obama. She said that "we've got our eyes on you." That never hurts. My guess is that he makes more in one year than I have made in my entire working life. And I did OK. Oh, the fear! We all should be so scared.

So what are the facts on the ground in America? How do our fellow citizens – black, brown, "red," "yellow," tan, beige, and pinkish-white — get along with each other?

The Dusty Little Village – which actually harbors around 50,000 souls – is more truly "diverse" than any place most of the Virtue Signalers live. To my certain knowledge, we have no $15 million mansions here. Every spring, the graduation pictures of our students are run in the local paper, and it looks to be roughly divided in fourths in the incessant racial bean-counting. White students appear to have a slightly bigger "quarter," followed closely by Hispanic kids, then Indian kids, with African-American kids having the smallest "quarter." That is not a scientific head count, just eyeballing it. There are several different kinds of East Indians and Asian kids in the mix too.

But here's where it gets complicated: intermarriage is extremely common. Yes, all these ethnicities that allegedly hate on each other daily in a racist way seem to fall in love and marry or at least cohabit long enough to produce interesting offspring. If a baby's mother is black and Mexican and his father is Indian and Filipino, you tell ME what the hell "race" he is. And why it matters.

Here is just one day's observations at Copper Sky, our Intergenerational Community Center and gym. In one corner was a muscular young black trainer working with a middle-aged white woman. In another corner, a pregnant white woman was monitoring the sit-ups of an older black woman. The track on which I was trudging fatly along with my walking buddy is built over the basketball/volleyball court. Below us was an intense pickup basketball game of God knows WHAT races, only one kid identifiable as "black" and one as "white" and the rest various exotic mixtures. Oh wait…that blonde "white" kid up close has some "Asian" in him too. They were laughing, teasing each other, playing quite a physical style of the game, and not one person looked terrified or hateful. They might have even been (gasp) FRIENDS!

A limping older black gentleman, fresh from Physical Therapy, heard my walking partner say we had done 40 minutes, and he said, "Boy, I hope to reach your level some day…" which we both found to be a pathetically low bar, but nonetheless, sweet. We chatted with him a minute or two as we walked. Nobody was hostile or scared.

After our workout, my buddy gassed up his truck and headed for the cashier while I turned up the AC as high as it would go, even though it was only 118. A thin black teenager in a do-rag hit the store's door at the same time as my friend of even later middle age. The kid opened the door for him and also held it for a comely Mexican lass. Manners, nice!

Once, near home after a long road trip, I took a shortcut across Indian land and decided to gas up at the Indian gas station. As I approached the door of the attached convenience store, an Indian man, 30-ish, rushed and beat me to it. Silly me, I thought he was hurrying to open it for me. To my surprise, he butted ahead of me, opened the door JUST far enough for him to squeeze through and let it slam in my face. Way to stick it to "The Man," kiddo!

When I got inside the convenience store, I saw the Indian elders looking daggers at him. In every Indian culture with which I am familiar, elders are held in great respect, and there was no need for me to present ID to see that I qualified. I was not only a senior, and a lady, but a paying customer! The woman at the counter was clearly embarrassed. She said, “Sorry. Everybody thinks he’s a jerk.” Ah well. I was more sad than offended. Made it all the way home without any Play-Doh or my support otter. In fact, I’m going to bet that when the guy got home, he actually didn’t feel very good about himself. A conscience is a naggy thing.

Then last Saturday night, we drove 50 miles to a play in Peoria, AZ. Suburban Arizona – the EPICENTER of intolerance, if you believe our betters. We were very early and stopped into a dark little bar for a drink. Two large Mexican bartenders were tending to three lesbian couples, a heterosexual couple, two elderly black men (not together), and a couple of Jewish geezers of late, late middle age. Most of the others seemed to be regulars. Nothing but friendliness, laughter, generous pours, and a very loud jukebox that careened wildly between country and rap. Mr. AG put in the earplugs he carries all the time and nursed his double-Jack.

So how is our rainbow Family of Man doing? Pretty damn well, all slanderous accounts to the contrary. Absent the race hustlers and people for whom stirring the perpetual grievance pot is a lucrative career, most of us get along just fine. And that’s the truth.

ABOUT LAST WEEK'S DISGRACE

September 27, 2019

HEY, Remember the new Impeachable Crisis 3 or 4 Crises Ago? It's hard to keep up with the Impeachment Crisis du Jour, but I kind of took a mental health break and now want to comment on this old one, because it's so gosh-darn hilarious and right in my wheelhouse.

JUST when the Kavanaugh family thought it was safe for their children to watch television again, the fabulists came up with ANOTHER alleged Dangling Party-Penis with a young Brett K in the vicinity! Impeachment! Impeachment! Caw! Caw shriek the brain-dead buzzards, in search of carrion, several even with alleged law degrees. Evidence, schmevidence!

Free Range Penis 2.0 – now down the crowded rabbit hole along with Russian collusion -- is just another fairy tale by lying, deranged partisans intent on preserving full-term baby-killing and Constitution hating. Shameless Amy Klobuchar and the even crazier loons do not care if it happened or not. Amy is sitting at .001% traction in the Clown Candidate Olympics and needs something, anything, to get into the running, if not for President, maybe Vice President or Secretary of State, which worked out so well for Madame President, Hillary Rodham Clinton, who, based on polls the night before the election, won in an historic landslide.

If Bernie or Biden secures the job of losing to Trump, there will be a guaranteed spot on the Ticket of Futility for an Insufferable Designated Uterus. But, if Elizabeth War-Whoop gets the main nod, then the Uterus slot will be filled and Amy will be superfluous unless the Democrats want to eclipse the McGovern and Carter losses with an All-Female Ticket that includes one always-enraged fake Indian and one "Minnesota Nice" Party Hack who eats with a comb.

But back to the latest Kavanaugh smear. The Dangling Penis 2.0 sequel makes no sense whatsoever. Who are the Democrat operatives who invent these lurid tales? They seem to have no inkling about either basic anatomy or the actual mechanics of sex. Since the upbringing of the middle-aged scold crowd has been so lacking, let Mother Ammo Grrrll school you on how to respond to an unwanted unveiling of a distinguished member.

As I understand the breathless little stories, some students at Yale 35 years ago – let that sink in – 35 years ago! -- sat around drunk in somebody's dorm room, no doubt discussing Fellini films, avant-garde atonal music, and politics. Suddenly, one of the boys just willy-nilly took out his willy, and possibly also his nilly. No fanfare – no warning – just PLOP – here it is? Happens all the time. What to do?

Unless you WANT to participate in some kind of *menage a several*, when a fella's pants come off, and his undies along with them, that's a very big clue to find your hostess, thank her for the nice party, and walk back to your own dorm room. Ladies? Isn't that what YOU would do if things got out of – or into – hand? Just leave? There's never any mention in these creative tales of being held captive or the door being locked from the outside, despite some 600 jillion copies of 50 Shades of Gray being sold in America alone. Stand up. Stagger home. End of story. Also, make a memo to self: get new friends! And maybe drink less.

Ah, but no. In the latest incarnation, the icky boy then had a "friend" who placed the offending organ RIGHT INTO A POOR VICTIM GIRL'S HAND!! Well, I never! No, really. I NEVER saw or heard of such a thing ever happening at any party. But, if it had, and Victim hadn't taken the opportunity to flee, how about just a strong yank with your now-fullish hand? Might that not curb the miscreant's enthusiasm for indecent exposure?

Let's unpack the preposterous little tale, shall we? (Ann Coulter did a great job last week. I wrote this before I saw hers, swearsies.). There are never any chairs in dorm rooms, so likely the Victim is sitting on the floor possibly beside Dangle Boy. He takes out Mr. Happy and his friend – where? On the OTHER side of the girl? On the other side of HIM? – reaches up or across and somehow deposits the little critter into a woman's hand. (Go ahead. Get some friends. Try it. I'll wait…) No women point and laugh, scream or swear at the guy. No young gentlemen say, "Hey, Creep, put that thing away." Nobody leaves. And nobody remembers 35 years later! Works for me! Haha, I kid. Sorry, NOT CREDIBLE!

Oh sure, more credible than the Regular Friday Night HS Orgy and Drunken Gang Rape tale concocted by that Julie Sweathog girl and her co-creator, excellent Democrat Presidential timber, and perpetual CNN contributor, Michael Avenatti.

More credible than a homely 15-year-old who was the only girl at a "party" with the drunk Cool Boys 2 years older, being mauled briefly when she went upstairs to potty. She has no idea where the party was, whose house, how she got there or how she got home. Clear that she only had the one beer, though, and that it traumatized her for life.

More credible than Ms. Ramirez after 6 days of relentless coaching and God knows what remuneration, remembering the Dangly Bit in the Face 1.0. And now this Traveling Penis 2.0 story. Why now? Well clearly, there is inside info on health prospects for RBG, may she live and be well. The ruthless, relentless, America-Hating Democrat Party which wishes every Trump voter dead has to send a message to future candidates for the Supreme Court: "Play ball or we will destroy you and humiliate your families. No lie is too absurd.

None."

Here should be the new rules going forward to put an end to these decades-old ludicrous accusations. Start with the investigators, the stinking hypocrites in Congress. Publish every lurid detail of every sealed "settled" sexual harassment claim funded by us taxpayers on behalf of the arrogant deviates and degenerates.

Then investigate the Megaphone Crowd. Have thorough investigations into the sex lives of every single journalist and media exec, black and white, male and female, gay and straight, going back to middle school, including forensic yearbook analysis, interviews with attendees at every single party they were ever at, any dance club, rave, etc. We deserve to know the purity of those hurling all those stones. AFTER a thorough and fair look at the glass houses of the people who have access to limitless stones, then the rules change to the following:

Statute of Limitations for bringing ANY charge of a sexual nature: one month. And that must include a police report. No "Tom Brokaw kissed me on a couch 50 years ago" crap any more. Enough. Sick to death of weaponized, unprovable fantasy porn? Yeah, #MeToo.

OCTOBER THRU DECEMBER

The Third Quarter opens with the first October column addressing conservatives' battle fatigue in light of the relentless attacks on President Trump and his supporters (us) building up to the next column and the Left's obsession with the fruitless impeachment drive. From there we discuss the wonderful windfall $50,000/month job of the fabulously-qualified Hunter Biden. And, some timely travel tips.

November columns begin with a few observations on the occasion of my 73rd birthday. You have probably heard the great Merle Haggard song, "Always on a Mountain When I Fall"? And such is life, mine at least. I went from one week's joyous celebration of the anniversary of my birth to a column about my first (and please, God, my only) scorpion sting. Which occurred – why not? – the NIGHT BEFORE I was slated to take off on yet another road trip to see my Papa in his Assisted Living Facility in Minnesota. Adventures ensue, winding up with a Thanksgiving ode to gratitude for ALL my blessings upon my return.

December begins with another Hunter Biden column – the gift that keeps on giving – in a piece called "Four People More Qualified than Hunter Biden" for his job. Another column marks the kick-off of the legendary Biden "No Malarkey" tour. The final column in 2019 and the end of the Third Quarter is a review of the film "Midway". Whew!

RESISTANCE, RESILIENCE AND BATTLE FATIGUE

October 4, 2019

On my earliest report card, my kindergarten teacher had already spotted a pint-sized manic-depressive: "Little Susan is very easily elated or depressed," she wrote in 1951. Luckily, most of the time I was – and still am – elated. In a manic phase, you wouldn't even BELIEVE what can be accomplished, especially paired with a touch of OCD.

So though I may be more prone to depression than some, I sense that many of us cannot get our heads around all that has been thrown at our President and, by extension, against us Deplorables. It's a relentless, coordinated, and tedious coup attempt. This week I turn 73, and I have never seen anything like this in my long life. Sometimes even a normally cheerful person can get towed under from the never-ending tsunami of lies.

WE MUST NOT LET THAT HAPPEN! When our hateful and humorless overlords try to make us too depressed to fight back, joy becomes a revolutionary act.

It often seems that the forces of totalitarianism have all the weapons – every single television network, except for a few programs on Fox (Tucker, Laura, Sean), every newspaper, Hollywood, sports, education, woke corporations, and the powerful tech billionaires. Why not just give up? We have Rush (an army of one, bless him), and a few great bloggers. And, oh yeah, millions of the most productive, smart, useful, independent and patriotic Americans.

We can't give up because we owe it not just to our children and grandchildren to fight, but to the ones who came before who pledged their lives and treasure in order to bequeath us the miracle of opportunity and liberty we have inherited. Because the Education Establishment presents American history as one long bleak opportunity for icky white people to oppress everyone in sight, it is incumbent on the rest of us to set the record straight.

How many young people understand how perilously close the American Revolution came to being crushed by the foremost military power in the world at that time? For the first part of that brutal 8-year war against England, General Washington spent most of his time trying to keep the Continental Army together, disciplined, fed, shod, and on the run to avoid being wiped out. Though a decisive victory would not come until 1781 at Yorktown, early on he won a couple of important battles in New Jersey, including, of course, the famous crossing of the Delaware to surprise and kill or capture the Hessian mercenaries.

The Brits and Hessians thought the ragtag bunch of American colonists were an unprofessional army of Deplorable upstarts. They were the first to disparage what might then have been called "Ride-Over Land." Big mistake. The commander of the Hessians, Col. Johann Rall, had 36 years in as a professional soldier. His troops let down their guard and – as the iconic joke poster with Washington crossing the Delaware says – "America! We will cross a frozen river in a blizzard, sneak up on you and kill you. On Christmas!"

And they did! It was a tremendous morale-booster to an army making bloody footprints in the snow with rags tied around their bare feet. The Hessians' rout netted food, boots, and munitions which gladdened the hearts of these winter soldiers, and spurred enlistments.

Our enemies, foreign and domestic, CONSTANTLY underestimate us due to their own bigotry, as we saw as recently as 2016. One more example, this time from World War II – at the bloody slaughter at Guadalcanal, the Japanese were undone in part by their racism. They were assured that the American fighting man was a coward and would turn tail and run when attacked. The Japanese repeatedly charged that "misunderestimated" bunch of sissies, the United States Marines Corps. It did not go well. The Japanese lost 31,000 men.

If you want to read an informative, heart-stopping account of many critical battles of both World Wars, order our friend Tony Peluso's spellbinding novel, *Waggoners Gap*. He wrote it over a 10-year period as a debt of honor and gratitude to one of his unnamed heroes. Tony's great page-turner is part scrupulous history, part sexy potboiler, and part a multi-generational immigrant family saga. Read it to remind yourself what has been paid in blood and what is owed those heroes, living and dead. I know many of you are knowledgeable history students of all things military. This is a unique one to add to your collections.

It's long – hey, it's our Tony! – but I devoured all 600 pages in two days, barely remembering to breathe for several pages of some battles. I cried often. It is an inspirational spine-stiffener for these difficult days. Hard not to say, "If that guy can take out five Germans while sustaining three wounds, I bet I can at least send a check or put up a yard sign."

There are plenty among PL's readers who have served, God bless you every one. We count on you to teach the rest of us to hang tough. Eric Swalwell looks forward to nuking us. ALL the Democrat candidates for President have pledged to take our guns. They ALL raised their hands for FREE medical care for illegals, FREE college, REPARATIONS for almost everyone except you, and FREE, unlimited abortion. And that's just their warm-up act. What to do, friends, besides fight like hell to see that DJT wins in 2020? Here are my recommendations to help stay both sane and steadfast through our long, righteous fight:

DISCONNECT SOMETIMES. If the Internet is just bringing you down and every channel, including sports and Animal Planet are bellowing "Orange Man Bad," turn them all off. Read a book, embroider a pillow with Yoda on it that says, "Offended you are? A bleep I don't give." Watch a clean, funny, not deranged comic like Jim Gaffigan, Nate Bargatze, or Brian Regan. Bake something wonderful. Go to the gun range for some "Group Therapy."

CONNECT: Call a like-minded friend; go for a walk with a buddy. Get outside yourself and visit a nursing home, VA Hospital, or just your mother, if you are blessed still to have one.

PLAY: A board game with grandkids, a musical instrument, your favorite upbeat music. Dance like nobody is watching; even though they ARE and are making fun of you. Replay every 2016 election YouTube video predicting an historic sweep by Hillary, and the aftermath with the caterwauling losing losers who lost, especially the totally unbiased media. Never gets old!

PRAY as hard as you have ever prayed for anything. Read the Psalms. Do not let the Democrats as constituted ever have power again. This time the leftists haven't even pretended to promise "If you like America, you can keep America." They hate it. And us.

CONSCIOUSNESS OF GUILT

October 11, 2019

Once, when I was a small child around 4, an idea came to me to cut two little round holes in my sheer white bedroom curtains. I didn't say it was a GOOD idea. Apparently, it was not my first bad idea involving a scissors as I have the one and only formal childhood portrait of myself, about age 3, wherein I had helpfully cut my own bangs the day before the sitting.

But, having cut two hunks out of the curtains, I had an unanticipated problem. What to do with the evidence? Ah, another cunning idea came to me – I would hide the little round doughnut holes in one of my Golden Books. Mother noticed the mutilated curtains more quickly than I had anticipated: "SUSAN MARIE, come in here! Who in the world cut holes in your curtains?!!" Now, I have to confess here that I am a terribly bad liar. This deficiency definitely impaired my ability to be a career criminal or politician (BIRM).

And I had been very strictly inculcated from birth – much like George Washington, only much shorter – not to lie. What's a 4-year-old miscreant to do? Deny, deny, deny all the while being careful not to lie directly. Start by throwing a pal under the bus. "Maybe Libazeth Brauer did it?" Mother pointed out that Elizabeth hadn't been over for many days and just yesterday the curtains were fine. She also noticed the scissors on the chair NEAR the curtains. (Doh!) They were blunt, plastic kids' scissors. Frankly, I don't know how they even managed to cut the curtains. (Why didn't we have commonsense scissor control to prevent inanimate objects from causing tragedy?)

"You know who I think cut the curtains?" Mama asked. "I think you did it, didn't you?"

"That is not in my purview," I parried. No, wait, I didn't say that. I said, "I did it on accident." (Happens all the time. Well played!) A few days later, she was reading me a Little Golden Book and out fell the two little round cut-outs. I burst into tears of contrition – but mostly tears of being caught – and took the only course left to me: I opened an impeachment "inquiry" into Mama. No, again, that is incorrect. I said, "Let's not tell Daddy, Ok?" She agreed.

And with a mighty leap, we transition from a totally-guilty 4-year-old's dilemma to the current Democrat Party's reaction to being caught flat-footed with their leading candidate bragging about being a nepotistic crook and influence peddler, and yukking it up with the Foreign Relations Committee. The bald-faced nature of the quid – "Let the Ukraine pay for Hunter's cocaine!" – in exchange for the quo – a BILLION (with a B) dollar loan blew my naïve little mind. It turns out that I AM still capable of being shocked!

I have never in my life been more ashamed of ever voting Democrat than I am today. Ditto for voting for the pathetic Mitt Romney, who has never once even pretended to have the President's back, except as a place to plunge a shiv. Come ON, Utah! He cannot possibly reflect your values. Yeah, he shares your religion. Big deal. Jerry Nadler, Chuck Schumer, and Bernie Sanders ostensibly share mine, but I would sooner vote for a conservative atheist, any baby-protecting Born Again Christian, or a border-defending Rastafarian than any of them.

A more venal Democrat collective of kleptocrats, liars, hysterics, and narcissists I have not seen in my many decades on the planet. Whenever they are caught, they go on hysterical offense, enlist their ventriloquist's dummies in the media, get Hollywood twits to twitter and start screeching "IMPEACHMENT" as a really boring, yet threatening, mantra.

Even before the inauguration, the Democrats have played non-stop, Impeachment Whack-A-Mole. RUSSIAN COLLUSION! (WHACK! – none.) Well, okay, then, OBSTRUCTION of the investigation of a non-crime! (WHACK – did not happen.) RAAACISM! (WHACK! Lowest unemployment among blacks and Latins in history!). Trump won't give us the transcript of the Ukraine phone call! (WHACK!) I got your transcript right here! (WHACK!)

I hated the stupid Whack-A-Mole game at Chuck E. Cheese, where I spent several thousand expensive hours when my son was young. It was a futility in which you could not win because the moles just kept popping up no matter how many times you whacked them.

The bottom line is this: 2016 was not supposed to happen. They were supposed to get eight more years to "fundamentally transform" America into The Venezuela of El Norte. Hillary was going to win in a landslide. Open borders, felony voters, cemetery registration, vote harvesting and eliminating the electoral college would guarantee Democrat wins forever. No need even to start shredding damning evidence in every department, because… SAY WHAT? She LOST!!! Order Bleach Bit by the gallon and call Mad, Mad Maddow STAT!

The shredding machines must have been running full-time, 3 shifts, until January 20th, and even then the Swamp was so laden with spies, leakers, rogue Intelligence thugs, hacks in black, GOP obstructionists and Never-Trumpers, that Trump — who thought he had seen everything in the comparatively fair-playing, courteous worlds of New York real estate, the construction industry and reality television — was initially caught off guard.

And always with the tedious invective dialed up to Eleven. Once "Nazi" and "Hitler" come out, there's really no place else to go. Mao and Stalin made Hitler look like a piker, but the people shrieking at Trump will never admit it. Hey, communism is all in a good cause; gotta break a few eggs. Icky White People, Asians, Conservatives of Color — no omelet for you!

Hysteria that constant and that over-the-top meant only one thing to me – there were legions of people who were guilty as hell and terrified of losing everything, including their liberty. My old Irish grandfather once said the following to my cousins and me when we loudly denied tossing the barn cat into the stock tank to see if it could swim*: "You throw a stone into a pack of dogs, and the one that barks the loudest is the one you hit." To call the current Democrats a pack of dogs is an insult to rabid dingos everywhere, but you take my point.

*The cat COULD swim, but evidently, did not enjoy it. We COULD run from Grandpa. But not fast enough as it turned out. In our defense, we were free range kids, left unsupervised. Also, we were 4, 5, and 7. Plus, the cat started it.

THAT IS A WHEELBARROW FULL OF MONEY!!

October 18, 2019

Okay. I stipulate to the fact that geezers are always comparing the cost of things today with the prices (and values) of things when we were young, and I identify as a geezer.

We used to make fun of Mama. "Yes, Mother, we realize that bread was a nickel, but you had to work all day as a nanny for a dime, and you only got half a sandwich for your lunch. We get that. But, really, the movie is 15 cents and everybody is going to Tammy and the Bachelor, so please, please, please could you look in your purse and see if you have a dime and a nickel? I have my own dime for popcorn. Unbuttered."

Just by the by, Mama really DID get a dime a day as a nanny (and "light" housekeeper) for her older and much richer first cousin in the Twin Cities the summer after high school graduation. And the cheap, lazy (bad word) really DID give her only half a sandwich to eat at noon while she herself went out with lady friends to fancy downtown restaurants. Nice.

That experience, told to me dozens of times, has made me very generous to my hired help, even though none of them are even related to me. Of my many faults, exploiting people who work for me is not one of them. Not to worry, though, because in her 50s through 70s, Mama earned the big bucks — $4.00 an hour to clean houses like, I guarantee you, they had never been cleaned before. With laundry. And windows.

My first job in my father's drugstore paid 65 cents an hour, and years later, $1.00 an hour. We worked a 6-day week, always and every fourth Sunday. On those occasions, that meant we worked 13 days in a row. The four drugstores also took turns being open until 9 p.m. which was a real treat as well. How I came to loathe the tourists who would drift into the store at 8:57 and just loiter about for 20 minutes, not buying anything! Were YOU ever in a drugstore at 8:57 p.m. in Alexandria, MN in the summers of 1962-66? If so, as the Yiddish curse goes: "May all your teeth fall out but one, and that one should ache you." Not that I'm still bitter.

When Mr. AG and I were first married, I worked for IBM as a typist for $400 a month. Every two weeks I took home $167.80 after taxes. We had no telephone and no vehicle. When we lived in San Francisco in the early 70s with a newborn, we earned $8,000 for the year. TOGETHER. STILL no car, although we did have a telephone, but – and I'm going to capitalize this so you know I'm yelling – WE DID PURCHASE BASIC CATASTROPHIC HEALTH INSURANCE! Always. Instead of, you know, drugs, tattoos or hair extensions.

Let me also make perfectly clear, as Nixon used to say, I did not at the time, and do not now resent at all that we did not have the income that others did who made better choices, including years more of study and sacrifice. Nearly all of Mr. AG's friends became doctors, lawyers or college professors with multiple Ph.Ds.

We were busy saving the world at that time and not only failing to earn much, but also being nagged incessantly into giving what little we did have to "The Movement." THAT I do resent, but, hey, we were adults and 100 percent responsible for these stupid choices. Sometimes in life, barring a straitjacket, nobody can prevent you from voluntary suckerdom.

Eventually, our silly political notions got smashed on the hard rocks of reality. We more or less caught up to most of our peers in financial comfort. Mr. AG earned a law degree plus developed expertise as an I.T. Guy. He really DID "learn to code." Add in my few lucky breaks as a comedian and our fortunes improved markedly. One equalizer, of course, was that we stayed together for half a century, while some of our peers had to divide their assets in half, sometimes more than once. Another was that we were blessed with good health – Baruch Hashem (thank God) and kinahora (a Jewish incantation to turn away the Evil Eye). Also, nobody ever had a substance abuse problem, not counting Krispie Kremes.

Which brings me to my actual point. For weeks now, I have been trying to get my mind around the 50 THOUSAND dollars A MONTH that Hunter-Gatherer Biden got for NOTHING except the obvious connection to his Daddy. I mean, am I the only one who thinks that is a LOT of money? What COULD you do to earn that? Especially when you don't speak the language, and have no expertise either in the country or the industry for which you are "consulting." Could it BE any clearer?

After many decades on this corrupt planet, you expect some gouging, some kickbacks, some bribery called by nicer names like "finders fees," "closing costs" or "resort fees" in hotels that provide things like kayaks and hang gliding that the Vasses are never going to use but are forced to pay for. A little "taste," as they say in certain circles, as part of doing a deal is expected. But 50 thousand dollars A MONTH??? I mean how did the Bidens settle on that amount? Was that just Hunter's regular coke budget for a month?

ONE month in my 30-year comedy career, I actually did make $50,000. (It was in an October, always my busiest booking month; honest to God, the following July, I made $1500.) Such are the vagaries of the comedy business. Makes budgeting and estimated taxes a joy.

Anyway, I made that $50,000 by a freakish booking schedule that just fell into place like God Himself was my agent. A client would call to check my availability for the second week, say, and it would turn out that their event was on the only night of that week that I wasn't booked. Sure, it meant one night in Mississippi and the next noon in Oregon, and an evening show in Texas, but it could theoretically be done! I remember that for that pathetic July I got just five total inquiries – every blessed one for July 29th! What were the chances? As regular readers know, I hate flying; that lucrative October I had 29 flights in 31 days. In other words, I WORKED for it and so hard that I got viral pneumonia. The whole month I never had a wakeup call later than 4:00 a.m. to make another dreadful germ-laden flight.

So the idea that someone could get that for doing absolutely nothing and month after month for YEARS makes me want to puke. And with OUR tax dollars – a billion of them — as the humungous prize for the bribe. And he and his Daddy walk free. Sad. Not quite as evil as a PALLET of American greenbacks to the hostage-taking terrorists in Iran, but dang close. These are greedy, sleazy, evil people. Not one of whom will ever do a day of time. Convince me I'm wrong.

TRAVEL LESSONS

October 25, 2019

Democrats have achieved maximum lunacy (so far), so it's time for another mental health break while we ponder how and why President Trump is making fat black women so fat. No, really. He has been "credibly accused" of that by a fat black woman. With a big fat Ph.D. If he can make unhinged Jewish women fat — Bette Midler and Babs Streisand say he has force-fed them like a pate-bound goose liver – it would be racist not to make black women fat, too.

So let us leave crazy talk, and let me give you some advice about road trips instead. I have heard recidivists brag that they know how to "jail." Well, after 30 years on the road, I know how to "hotel." Let's start with the Mundane and move on to the Wise and Important.

Does it get any more "mundane" than toilet paper? Now, I have not stayed in the Georges Cinq in Paris, where 30 years ago I read that the rooms STARTED at $1,000 a night. So, it's possible that when you are paying that amount, corporate management chooses to spring for a second ply. (On the other hand, it's FRANCE, so who knows?) But I can assure you that even in some of the mid- to luxury-level properties in the U.S.of A, the toilet paper is pathetic.

You can almost hear the conversation between the hotel purchaser and the paper goods wholesaler: "Yeah, this one-ply tissue paper seems nice, but it's more than I was hoping to spend. Do you happen to have anything both thinner and rougher? Maybe something in your sandpaper line? Rough, but you can still SEE through it? Is there a half-ply brand?" For this reason, I always bring my own favorite toilet paper. (Charmin Ultra-Soft.)

Our friends Margie and Don, world-class hosts of the lovely lake home in southern Minnesota, have top-notch toilet paper which they jokingly claim they dole out two to a guest to limit the scope of the visit. When you're out of Charmin, you're out. A reasonable policy. Otherwise, you might be tempted to stay the entire summer…which is our plan for next summer. Shhh…it's going to be a surprise! We plan to eat no fiber and drink no liquids and make those 4 rolls last the entire summer. Who needs both kidneys anyway? I mean, Margie is a great cook, and she and Don have a Jet Ski AND a speedboat; it's a no-brainer…

Here's another thing: hotels expect – generally correctly – that most guests are going to use their hotel rooms for two things, one of which is sleeping. Neither activity requires bright light. However, when your hotel room is your "home away from home" for, say, two weeks while visiting your Papa, lighting becomes more important. I often bring 60 watt bulbs, paper plates, napkins and plastic silverware, so that we can take leftovers from restaurants and reheat them in the microwave. Two meals for the price of one! Amortize, amortize!

Some of your finer hotels will provide upscale shampoos and lotions, sadly soon to be illegal in California. It's tacky to steal extras from the maid's cart – and the whole world has security cameras now — but if you tip generously, sometimes several extras will just appear. Once when I treated my parents to two nights at the Ritz Carlton in Naples, Florida when they accompanied me on a gig there, Mother managed to charm the maids enough to make off with a good starter kit for her own boutique.

Also, if you are over the age of consent, never look in the giant magnifying makeup mirror in the bathroom. Especially if you tend to depression and are traveling with a weapon. One small chin hair looks like the rope you climb in gym.

GOOD IDEAS ON THE ROAD

Be open to spontaneity and adventure! Talk to EVERYONE. People are incredibly interesting. I have had great conversations with a Muslim housekeeper who was fasting for Ramadan and a Vietnam vet who had fostered 24 troubled kids; a Pakistani hotelier during a tornado in Guthrie, Oklahoma, and an Indian waitress in the White Buffalo Bar in the Gage Hotel in Marathon, Texas, to mention just four out of a thousand fun conversations on the road.

From just opening up a conversation with strangers, we have had the opportunity to attend a Bat Mitzvah party in a hotel in Amsterdam, and a pro basketball game in Israel with an Iraqi Jew. In Columbus, MS, a businessman in line at the coffeeshop was embarrassed by the curt response by the young barista to my request for bottled water and led me back to his store, introduced me to his entire sales staff and gave me water. I bought several dresses. Win-win.

SMALL SETBACKS WILL OCCUR. STAY COOL.

On our recent summer trip, I was flying along, making good time, when I heard some kind of No Good Very Bad Terrible noise underneath the car. I assumed a tire had blown and by the grace of God, there was Exit 120, so I pulled off. It was not Arizona hot, but Iowa hot in July was plenty toasty enough. Mr. AG discussed our situation with AAA for many long sweaty minutes. The Customer Service Rep promised a tow truck would be there within 45 minutes. I had personally heard Mr. AG say very clearly at least three times the name of the Highway, the name of the Exit and the make, model and color of the vehicle.

When asked for the fourth time the color of the car, I had to stifle a laugh when he said calmly, "Tell you what. Just have them tow ANY random 2018 Genesis with two people in it that they see parked on the shoulder of the off ramp of Exit 120." Haha. Mr. AG, also known as Max Cossack, is quite the card who writes very funny novels you might enjoy.

At last a great guy (and Trump supporter) appeared in the world's oldest, dirtiest, smokiest, but extremely welcome, tow truck and took us back to the Hyundai dealer in Council Bluffs. It turned out to be the cover over the oil pan thingy – okay, I'm not a motorhead – that had popped out, and was dragging, making a horrendous racket. Fixed in about 30 minutes and back on our way. Experienced quite the feeling of déjà vu retracing our miles. Both ways.

UNRELATED RANDOM THOUGHTS AND PIPE DREAMS

In Del's Restaurant in Tucumcari, New Mexico (highly recommended), we saw a table of bikers who were three of the hugest men I have ever seen. Not fat either – evidently Trump's be-fattening wiles don't work on bikers — solid muscle. Where's Antifa when these guys are around? Even the ladies with them could take the little Antifa soy-boys. If one of these men barely tapped a lock-wielding masked Antifa woman-like substance, he would perform an unauthorized splenectomy. After watching the disgusting violence that was encouraged and enabled by the Democrat government in Minneapolis during President Trump's recent rally there, a Grrrll can dream.

WHAT THE HECK? ANOTHER BIRTHDAY?

November 1, 2019

Last month's birthday wasn't one of the "0" or "5" birthdays that we seem to think more significant. I'm just happy to still be here at 73. Two of my lifelong friends the same age are not. Most of you already wished me Happy Returns a couple of weeks ago, so I'm not angling for more good wishes. It's just an excuse to lighten up and muse about a few minor cultural changes from our childhood to our geezerhood. I eagerly await your contributions.

I am an avid collector of humorous refrigerator magnets. One of my current favorites features a little old lady saying: "I'm so old, I can remember going through a whole day without taking a picture of anything."

If that's not one of THE most striking differences, I don't know what is! Photographs, up until the magical Polaroids, had to be taken, then remain in the Brownie until you finished the film, which could take YEARS, then developed at a drugstore or camera shop, then picked up. There were inevitably several shots that were either repetitive or terrible, but you had to pay for them anyway. You threw them in a shoebox and years later nobody had any idea who some of the people were or where they were or why there was a photo of the occasion.

Firstborns, such as myself, had more photos taken of them than subsequent siblings, and even those usually contained the oldest child as well. An Orthodox friend of mine, number 9 of 11, told me that when she had to have a baby photo for a school project, her mother dug through the shoeboxes, produced a cute baby, and said, "Here. I think this might be you." Catholic and Mormon kids can relate.

Last spring I was at a Diamondbacks game where the woman in front of me took 75 pictures of her very adorable toddler in the 5 innings she lasted in the game. The child, obviously an old hand at this, happily struck a pose for each shot. Is this a good thing?

Another magnet shows a chipper young woman saying, "I just saved $2000 a week by making my own coffee at home!" If you could bring back my Grandma – who drank a couple of POTS of coffee a day – and tell her that someone would happily pay over $5.00 for one cup, she would faint dead away. The RENT on their share cropper farmhouse was $8.00!

I had friends who had serious meltdowns about aging as early as 30. The only number that ever bothered me was 50. I went into a brief tailspin realizing that even if I lived to 99 – unlikely – more than half of my life was gone. When I hit 51, I thought, "Hey, now I'm just in my EARLY 50s. It's all good." Hard to grasp that that minor "crisis" was almost a quarter century ago! And I am happier and more at peace with myself now than at any time in my life. Which I might as well be, because I have no choice!

It is a notorious trait of the "late, late middle agers" to long for the "good olde days," some of which may not have been as good as we remembered. (World Wars, Depression, the Klan, no deodorant, no Keurig, no Chick-fil-A, etc.) But it sure is tempting and fun to reflect on what was considered normal back in the day.

I was still raised in the era of radio. Jack Benny and *Gunsmoke* were fabulous on the radio. Mother and I listened to her "stories" – Helen Trent and Ma Perkins – as we did dishes. The theme song for Helen Trent ("Can women 35 and over still find love?") was "Juanita." I can still hum a few bars if you'd like. It was very dramatic, like the story itself.

Men wore suits and fedoras to everything from church to ballgames. Grownups looked like grownups and children looked like children. No grown men wore torn jeans and t-shirts unless they were doing manual labor or fishing. No little girls wore shorts with "Juicy" on their bottoms. Farmers sweating in the fields in the '50s dressed better than today's guests at weddings and funerals! Grandma did hundreds of hours of gardening in a calf-length cotton "housedress," a slip, corset, nylons, and old leather shoes. Also a sunbonnet.

I keep reading that the Kid Culture we grew up with is utterly dead. Few little ones know "Ring Around the Rosy" or "Duck, Duck Grey Duck" or "Red Rover" or "Kill the Man with the Ball." You would have to pry their phones or game devices out of their sticky little hands and try to force them outside. God forbid, grade-schoolers today would ever play Mumblety-Peg which involved an actual working jackknife, or just wander around with a .22 rifle shooting at random stuff in a junkyard. Heck, Dodgeball and Tag are now all but illegal. A "gun" chewed out of the bologna in a sandwich for sure is illegal and cause for expulsion.

One of the truest tests of how old you are is in the area of names. My freshman year at Northwestern (1964) there were 4 "Susans" out of 30 girls on my floor. Now the name is in that kind of limbo – not quite old enough to be cutely retro (like Gert and Emma), but too unhip to be kewl, along with Jane, Joan, Jean, Kathy, Carol, and Linda.

Almost all adults smoked. My paternal grandfather had been smoking since age 9. When his beloved wife of 53 years passed away, he asked to visit my parents for a few weeks. When they arrived to pick him up, he had been waiting for hours on the screened-in porch in his good brown suit, tie, and hat with the suitcase his wife had always packed for him. Mother picked up the suitcase and thought it felt a little light, but didn't investigate further. It turned out to contain three white handkerchiefs and two cartons of Camels. No jammies, no undies, no socks, no second outfit. But he had the important stuff!

We had two functioning political parties that put forth their ideas and candidates and nobody rioted in idiotic masks if their candidate lost. My family was rock-ribbed Republican but when Jack Kennedy won in 1960, not a single "comedian" carried a bloody, beheaded likeness of him as a joke. No "right-winger" advocated raping Jackie or putting John-John in with pedophiles; no woman "comic" called anyone in the Kennedy family a "feckless c***." No short, ugly has-been actor said "F*** Kennedy" at the Oscars. Any of these scenarios was absolutely unthinkable.

The political competition was over which party could claim to represent and to love America the most. Good times, good times. Ah, how far we are down the Road to Perdition! I predict that 2020 will be a U-turn on Nonsense Highway and the grown-ups will be back in charge in the House. Please, God.

AMMO GIRL: 18; SCORPIONS: 1

November 8, 2019

Well, I suppose if you live in Arizona long enough, it is bound to happen. On the last Friday in October, just as Mr. AG was putting steaks on the grill for dinner, I ran out of paper towels and went to the utility closet for a new roll. I picked it up and immediately thought, "Who the heck [expletive inaccurate and incomplete] put a needle in the paper towels?"

But it very quickly was much worse than a needle prick. Much. Within minutes, I would have given ANYTHING for a good old-fashioned needle in the forefinger.

But, no. This was the dreaded scorpion sting, my first losing encounter with something that stings with a potent neuro-toxin.

My record had previously been approaching Bob Gibson's complete game stats in 1968 (28). In ten years, I had slain at least 18 scorpions in the house and garage. Most of them I found just ambling across the kitchen floor or SOMEHOW getting into a drawer in the bathroom vanity, to frolic among the backup face creams and hand lotions.

The first one I found in that drawer scared me so badly I initially considered shooting it, but rejected that option as overkill, not to mention worry about the ricochet and the dubious legality of firing a weapon in a house that belongs to an HOA. I believe the official cause of death was pulverization by deodorant can.

I even narrowly avoided disaster when I was doing yoga on my living room carpet and saw a teeny tiny critter scampering along the edge of my yoga mat. Without my glasses on I almost just swatted it, but something told me not to. It turned out to be a miniature scorpion. Whether a late, late middle-aged wives' tale or not, the tiny ones are reputed to be the worst stingers since they supposedly just fire ALL their toxins at the target while the larger ones are more restrained. That particular scorpion did not live long enough to develop restraint.

So back to the recent losing encounter. I precipitously dropped the roll of paper towels and the scorp fell off on the carpet, where Mr. AG attempted to kill it. It's not easy to kill a bug on deep-pile carpeting, even if you weigh 178 lbs. (Mr. AG, not me. Yet.) I made Mr. AG kick it from the carpet where it wouldn't die to the tile where it blew itself up along with 3 of its children. No wait, that was something else. It landed on the nice hard tile where I could grind it into dust. Not that I hold grudges.

Meanwhile, Mr. AG got on the phone to Poison Control where a nice lady asked me if I was having any difficulty breathing. I said "No" and she said, "You probably won't die from this." While that might have reassured a less congenitally anxious person, I said, "Define 'probably.'" She told me that a scorpion sting is actually a puncture wound that should be washed with soap and water. She then asked about my level of pain on a scale from one to ten. At that juncture (or puncture, haha), it was only about a 7, but the neurotoxin had already started to spread up my forefinger to my hand, which I took to be a bad sign.

She then recommended a booster tetanus shot "within the next few days." Since I was leaving in the early morning on yet another road trip to Minnesota to see Papa, delay was not an option. We set off for our Fairly Urgent Care facility, only about two miles away. By this time, it was about 20 minutes before full sunset and the blazing Arizona sun was right in our eyes such that two reasonably intelligent adults who had each been to this Urgent Care before sailed right by it and promptly got lost. Me, I would expect this to happen, but Mr. AG has a great sense of direction. We developed a new sympathy for baseball players who miss routine flies because they "got lost in the sun."

Eventually, with the aid of both phone GPS and a call to the facility, it turned out to be about 100 feet from where we were standing. Oy. There were only two patients ahead of us. A sweet young man who could have been Doogie Howser's kid brother came in and assured me that the "discomfort" from the toxin usually wore off in 6-12 hours. Evidently, the medical profession has done studies in which saying the word "pain" makes suggestible patients believe that something hurts. They love words like "discomfort" and "contraction" in the case of labor pain.

By this time, the discomfort had spread from my hand and up my arm all the way to my elbow. He asked again about the scale from 1 to 10. I said, "Doc, imagine that your skin has been flayed from the tips of your fingers up to your elbow. And then you are bathed in Tabasco Sauce. What number would you assign to that discomfort? Because, I think we're going to need more than 10."

Oh, but we're not really done yet. Because then you have to remember how it feels when your leg falls asleep and when it "thaws" out, it gets all tingly and prickly and sensitive. Yeah, add that sensation in along with the excruciating pain. That lasts for about 36 hours, give or take.

Our dear friends John and Angela and the Paranoid Texan were slated to come over to the patio for our Welcome Back First Gracious Living Fest. Yes, I felt less than festive, but I decided I could be miserable without company or distracted with loved ones around. And alcohol. Angela asked me what pain drugs they had given me and when I told her I had only been offered a tetanus shot, she said, “That’s not the remedy I PERSONALLY would have chosen for severe pain. No mention of Percocet or Vicodin?”

The good news is that the worst of it did pass in about 12-18 hours, although many of those hours occurred during alleged sleep time which was decidedly impaired. All of it ended in 36 hours. The less than good news is that the nurse with the full-sleeve tattoos told me that sometimes people get diarrhea from the tetanus shot. I know people often eat breakfast while reading this column, so I will only say that stopping every 20 minutes will SERIOUSLY affect your ETA on a long trip. Does it sometimes feel to you, too – though you are showered with blessings most of the time – that God is just messin’ with your head?

Bottom line: I had been terrified of being stung. It finally happened. It was not pleasant, but was of short duration and without lasting consequences. I was also told that any repeat episodes did not have cumulative effects. All good to know. Then the Paranoid Texan told me of a woman who had been stung IN THE NOSTRIL!! Extremely ungood. If you must be stung, I highly recommend that you try your best for an extremity.

A HIGH-STRUNG GRRRLL ON A HIGH-STRESS ROAD TRIP

November 15, 2019

Okay. So, when last we left our brave if slightly anxious and forgetful columnist, she had just been stung by a scorpion, had somehow managed to acquire a couple of hours' sleep, and was taking off by the dawn's early light for Highway 10 East, hoping to reach Minnesota before it snowed. Remember, kids, it was still only late October. "Winter," if you check your calendar, officially begins on December 21, some 8 weeks down the icy road, but winter in Minnesota is not bound by anything as silly and arbitrary as a calendar.

Can anything get worse than a trip that begins with a scorpion attack? Hold my beer. You've heard the description of an event or project being "snakebit." Well, praise the Lord and pass the ammunition, there was no snake involved, but the scorpion was not a good harbinger.

My intention is always to get through El Paso on either a Saturday or a Sunday. Weekdays, anytime within two hours of what is laughingly called "rush" hour, are out of the question. Going through El Paso – much like Texas itself – you THINK you are done, but there's always MORE of it. This being a Saturday, I fairly flew through El Paso, sometimes at speeds approaching 40 miles in a single hour! Several feet of road construction had been completed since my last trip through in July.

A couple of hours later found me in Van Horn, Texas, checked into my hotel and enjoying Pecan Crusted Salmon at the lovely restaurant in the El Capitan hotel. So far, so good. The scorpion sting on my forefinger only hurt now when I pressed on it, so, of course, I did that with some regularity. WHY do we do that? "Whoa, this canker sore hurts! Let me stick my tongue in it and see if it still hurts NOW, several minutes later. Yup, still does!"

The next morning at 6:15 when I made a beeline for the Holiday Inn Express Cinnamon Rolls and filled my travel mug with coffee, I was somewhat startled to notice that it was DARK. Yeah, I know, you guys already knew that. But, see, I live in Arizona where we do not participate in Daylight Savings Time because we don't feel like it. Well, that and the fact that the last thing on God's Green Earth that Arizona needs from April to November is another hour of blazing sunshine. Also, we are way south in the time zone. When I walk at 6:30 in the morning in Arizona, it is at least partially light, soon to be both light and toasty warm.

Oh well, I thought. It will surely be light soon. Though black as pitch out, I headed for a gas station and then followed the signs "To 10 East." The sign pointed me to a frontage road with the promise that there would be an entrance to 10 East any minute. And perhaps there was. But I missed it in the dark.

Oh well, I thought again. I bet this frontage road will continue until there's another entrance down the line. And then I dropped a good 8 inches with a scrapey plop. Uh-oh.

I remembered that our son had a little illustrated book by Shel Silverstein "Where the Sidewalk Ends" but I did not think he had written a companion piece, "Where the Frontage Road Ends." But end it did.

Ahead of me in my headlights was broken concrete like somebody had taken a jackhammer to it. Behind me was that 8-inch curb-like affair that I probably was not going to get back over in reverse. What to do? I had a blanket, sleeping bag, several loaded weapons, coffee, water, 16 rolls of toilet paper, and enough road snacks to last until Christmas, but the humiliation of being found there was too much to contemplate.

In the darkness, I saw that off to my left there was a flat patch of grass and a gentle slope UP back to a road where semis were zipping by. I assumed that that was Highway 10 East, or for sure some place better than where I was. I waited till I saw no semis in the right hand lane, gunned it and turned my 2012 Hyundai Sonata into an off-road all-terrain vehicle. Sometimes a grrrll has to do what a grrrll has to do.

It worked! Like several mistakes in life, sometimes you can't go forward and you definitely can't go backward, so you just have to chart "a whole nother" path, as we say in Minnesota.

I was pretty worried about the undercarriage, but – not to spoil the rest of the story – I have managed to drive it for over a week and hundreds of miles so far with no ill effects.

At one point I thought, "Oh, Lord, I smell gas!" And then I realized – idiot! — that I was in Midland/Odessa where the entire area smells like gas and oil because there are miles and miles and miles and miles of refineries. There are even dozens of those little bobbing donkey wells throughout the farmland and cotton fields.

It was dark until 8:15! I had cleverly left my Garmin in the trunk and was attempting to get to Guthrie, OK from some notes off an Internet map. Eventually, I stopped and fired up my Garmin. When you hear directions like "turn left at the place where the Johnson's barn burned down last spring," you know you are in the real boonies. I made that up, of course, but not by much. But Garmin Girl, scoldy "RECALCULATING!" wench that she is, did get me to Hwy 35 North, bless her heart. Once I get to 35N, I can practically drive it in my sleep. Probably have.

I stopped for a break, some great truck stop BBQ, and consulted Accuweather. Planning to overnight in my usual Marriott Courtyard in Ankeny, Iowa, I noticed it predicted up to 4 inches of snow there by afternoon. But nothing for further north. And so, I just kept driving. Seven hundred fifty miles, which I know ain't nuthin' to my many trucker fans, but a goodly piece, nonetheless. As I passed Ankeny, there was no snow – of COURSE, there wasn't! — but you can always count on southern Minnesota. For a nice band of about 50 miles it was dark, windy, and freezing cold with road construction and sleety, horizontal snow coming at me. And then I got through it and had only metro Twin Cities traffic to deal with, surprisingly heavy at 8:30 p.m. on a Monday night. Who ARE all these people, I wondered, and where are they going?

Well, I'm here now having twice daily visits with Daddy at his Assisted Living place. Yesterday we tried compression socks for the swelling in his ankles. I wish I had had video of the two of us trying to get them on him. Laughing that hard is good for you.

Maybe flying isn't so terrible after all. And I still have to get BACK. Where is St. Christopher when you need him? I heard he got demoted, but then reinstated like the planet Pluto, but Catholic sainthood lore is not really in my wheelhouse. TonyP? JimCR? Bueller? Any random practicing or lapsed but knowledgeable Catholic?

HIGHLIGHT REEL OF THE END OF THE ROAD TRIP!

November 22, 2019

One time in the Green Room of a Minneapolis comedy club, my colleague Sid came in from a round of golf. He was an excellent, almost-scratch golfer, a very smart guy, and funny comic. He said that a sudden squall had come up on the back 9 and he was almost hit by lightning. He said, "I was wearing my golf shoes, with my putter over my shoulder, and standing a few yards from a tree. When the bolt hit the tree, I thought, 'Have I left anything OUT that would guarantee my getting killed today?'" Luckily, he was spared that day.

But my, how often we do conspire to guarantee ourselves a bad outcome! This incident came back to me when I was trying to get to Wichita Falls, TX on my return trip from Minnesota. It was a sunny 77-degree day, the pavement was dry, there was little traffic. I was Cruise Controlin' at around 80 miles per hour. Suddenly, I was weaving and hearing that "woogedy, woogedy" sound as one travels over the metal warning strip just before you run out of asphalt. To the right was a fairly deep ravine.

Some people risk life and limb to pull a cat out of a burning building or hoist a car off an injured person. I imagined the scene when my dear husband, famous novelist Max Cossack, got the news of my turning my car into a crushed beer can suitable for the recycling bin:

Anorexic Woman News-Head with Frowny Face, hereinafter AWNHFF: So, Mr. Cossack, I am sorry for the loss of your wife, Sharon.

Max: Susan. Her name was Susan.

AWNHFF: Whatever. We just have 40 seconds here. Were the authorities able to determine what caused your wife to leave the road in such an unfortunate way?"

Max: Well, as near as they could tell, she seemed to be rooting through her large snack bag looking for a particular item. Our daughter-in-law said she gave her two Starbucks Cake Pops in St. Paul, and we could only find one half-eaten one at the bottom of the bag. She died with a stick in her hand, white frosting around her lips and sprinkles on her shirt.

AWNHFF: I see. I mean, I don't PERSONALLY see because I only eat kale, but I've heard of people being very fond of cake pops. At least she died doing what she loved.

Max: Yes. Her two main hobbies were snacking and hypochondria. In her personal papers she requested donations in her memory to Sickle Cell Anemia, Narcolepsy, Leprosy, Macular Degeneration, and Prostate Cancer.

AWNHFF: Was your wife a survivor of those diseases?

Max: No. My wife was a white woman with 20/20 vision who wasn't sick a day in her life. But those were just a few of the major things she worried about or looked up daily on WebMd. She figured if "men" could have periods, she could get prostate cancer.

AWNFF: Of course. Is there anything else you would like to add, Mr. Cossack?

Max: Yes. My books are for sale on Amazon and Jeffrey Epstein did not kill himself.

When one drives all day alone, you can see where the mind can wander. I DID get control of the car. Piece of cake, so to speak. And, in my defense, the cake pop was moist and chocolatey and, as mentioned, did have hard white frosting and sprinkles. I gently took the snack bag off my lap and did not root in it ever again unless stopped. Lesson learned.

SAVE YOURSELF TEN GRAND!!

I have previously mentioned the bizarre highway signs around road work in Oklahoma: “Slow down! Don’t hit our workers! Avoid a $10,000 fine!” Well, yes. That’s a pretty steep fine alright, but it would seem to me that the IMPORTANT thing, the truly CRITICAL thing is: “DON’T HIT A WORKER. THAT’S A HUMAN BEING!”

Which occasioned another flight of fancy in the form of an interior dialogue, the only kind I can have with no passengers in the car, the three hitch-hiking prisoners having begged early on to be returned to the relative safety of the penitentiary.

AG, phoning home: “Honey. It’s me. Listen, I’m in the middle of a spot of bother here, just outside Edmond and I wonder if you would mind bringing me $10,000.”

Mr. AG: “Good heavens! What happened?”

AG: “Well, it’s the darnedest thing. I didn’t FEEL like slowing down and I went and clipped one of the workers, a father of six, and…hello? Hello?”

Dialing my walking buddy, the Paranoid Texan. “Hey, remember that t-shirt we liked in that catalogue? — A friend will help you move, but a good friend will help you move a body — Oh, how we laughed and laughed! Well, you would not believe what just happened to me. So, if you could bring your pickup, a large carpet remnant, and a shovel…hello? Hello?”

TAKING UP RESIDENCE IN WICHITA FALLS, TX

Now at least I have hotel personnel to talk to, which is clearly an improvement from the voices inside my head. As reported, it was 77 when I arrived here. Somehow – don't ask me how, people I ask just say "Texas!"– it plunged overnight from 77 to 18 with freezing rain pellets and 400 mph winds (my own estimate, not official). I decided to stay on an extra day and write and sleep. Besides, I'm annoyed with Mr. AG for hanging up on me in my imaginary phone call. (Has anyone else ever been upset with their spouse all day for something they did in a dream?) Tomorrow will be better. I have put the snack bag in the trunk.

It is Veterans Day and I just listened to a moving and inspiring speech by the President. Every word about the veterans and not one word about himself. He is a better speaker than Obama by a country mile. Just one more thing for which he gets no credit.

MEDITATION ON GRATITUDE 2019

November 29, 2019

Yesterday, presumably, most of us ate beyond our fill of the traditional Thanksgiving fare. It is my favorite meal of the year. I particularly love stuffing – Heaven on earth! Whoever started the tradition of eating what is basically wet bread has a place in my heart forever. I tart my stuffing up with Cornbread, Hot Turkey Sausage, dried cranberries, chopped apples and pecans. And pile it on the dark meat turkey and bury it in gravy! (Sorry…I need a moment…)

One Thanksgiving, we hosted some nearly starved Jewish immigrants from the Ukraine. Sadly, they had not had the chance to apply for that $80,000 a month job that L'il Hunter snagged by the darnedest luck and his legendary expertise. When asked in the interview what he brought to the table in the way of credentials, he dusted off his nose, winked, and said, "Just BIDEN my time 'til I can turn into my favorite cowboy, The Loan A-Ranger, if you get my drift." They got it. They are corrupt, not stupid! His Daddy was so proud he bragged about his super-macho Godfather role in it.

Anyway, we taught our immigrant guests that the American way was to exclaim after the meal "I'm stuffed!" Not, "the gravy was so piquant," or "the turkey was so moist," but simply, "I'm stuffed!" Quantity rules the day; quality is merely a nice bonus. Shortly afterwards, the young husband ran into me at the market and said in his excellent but humorous English, "Oh, Shoshanna (my Hebrew name), you were most correct! My co-workers ask how was first Thanksgiving meal in America, and I say what you teach me – I was stuffed! – and they remark, 'How you know these words?'

When it comes to blessings, we Americans are all "stuffed." Anyone who says otherwise is a liar by the clock. Let me list just a few things that I am grateful for, in no particular order.

It all starts with family and I am profoundly grateful for mine. Depression survivors, my parents taught me how to do with less, how to do without, how to be really satisfied with what I had. There was never the slightest doubt that my parents loved me. I do know people whose parents were less demonstrative and, sadly, even some whose parents were abusive. These people had a harder row to hoe, but they developed strengths and coping strategies I do not possess. And virtually every one of them I know became terrific parents themselves.

In our late, late middle age years, it is difficult to make new friends. Old friends pass on at an alarming rate and established friendship groups can be hard to break into, as anyone who moves to a new town can attest. I am grateful for new friends I have made through this column. You know who you are. From Oregon to Florida, from Alabama to Massachusetts, from Washington to Montana, if I play my cards right, I should never have to stay in a hotel on the road again. Haha. I kid. I LOVE hotels. Marriott designates me "Titanium Elite," but I have invented my own special category I call Plutocrat Plutonium.

No words are adequate to describe how grateful I am to be an American with the boundless opportunity and freedom we all enjoy. The chic leftist hatred of America – with hatred of men and white people thrown in, because you just can't have too much hate! — is appalling. The Klown Kar of Kookoo Klepto Kandidates is making all manner of insane promises to bribe voters. Here's the only one I believe: they promise to take our guns, our private healthcare, and our money, and that they will do if they are able to cheat enough to win. The Democrats are always yapping on about "fighting for" the poor, never mind that virtually all their nostrums have made things infinitely worse. They are scared Schiff-less that if DJT gets four more years, there may BE no more poor! Who will need them then?

Odd as it may sound, I am grateful that my young husband and I had to struggle for many years. It is actually a blessing to be poor for a time – though it does get tedious if it goes on too long. It helps develop sympathy for people who have hit a rough patch economically, but it also makes you less impressed by the Permanent Professional Underclass, some of whom mightily resist any and all proven ways to improve their situation – work, save, don't do drugs, don't commit crime, get married, get some education. And work some more.

I am grateful for that husband mentioned above who, among many remarkable talents, understands our elaborate entertainment system of multiple remotes. I thank God for robust good health. And for the beauty of Nature. And the Second Amendment.

Lastly, I am grateful for cool gadgetry, especially my Keurig coffeemaker. One favorite morning ritual consists of whirling the little K-cup carousel and trying to decide which of several cute cups I will choose. Before Keurig, I had to perk a pot of pointless decaf for Mr. AG, put it in a thermos and then make my own. Now, I have one carousel for actual coffee and one for decaf, which frees up several extra minutes for me to sit and stare into space.

Though I am usually the last to adopt a new product or technology, I am a big fan of entrepreneurship and innovation, possible in the most encouraging and free economic environment in the world, not counting California. How well I remember the day that Mr. AG came home and announced that he had read about this great new musical innovation called "CDs." He declared that we were going to replace all our vinyl and tape! Seriously? The first large, clunky CD player we bought cost $600 and, at that moment in time, there were FIVE non-Classical CDs out. Within 6 months, you couldn't buy vinyl.

In the blink of an eye, I could buy my parents a boom box for $19.95, and find them World War 2 era songs on CDs in a big bin at Walmart for $5.00 each or less. Now, I am clearly the last person in America to still have a boom box and a vast collection of CDs. My "kids" synch up their fancy phones with the TV or car radio and play music in ways that elude me while they order coffee and cake pops with "apps" and we drive to pick them up and there they are! It's a brave new world for a mystified, resistant old lady. Ten years from now, I will write a column extolling this great new thing I've discovered called "Spotify." Haha. THAT will be long gone, too.

I thank the Power Line boys for giving me this space every Friday and thank all the delightful commenters who make Friday my favorite day of every week. Maybe because I am standup-trained, I am spoiled by having an audience react on the spot to my words and I really enjoy the back and forth with the commenters. To borrow from Dirty Harry Callahan, every Friday you "make my day." And if I live long enough, I will try every one of your recommended routes from Arizona to Minnesota. And back.

FOUR PEOPLE MORE QUALIFIED FOR THEIR LUCRATIVE NEW JOBS THAN HUNTER BIDEN – altogether a PARODY divided into 4 parts.

December 6, 2019

#1

Sean Spicer, fresh from what many called an "astonishing" run on Dancing with the Stars, has been tapped to choreograph and be principal dancer for the New York City Ballet Company!

"For $80,000 a month, I think I can bring a fresh perspective to the world of dance, call it an 'Everyman' kind of Dad Bod look in tights, not seen since the manly dance moves of, say, Rudolph Nureyev, whom I somewhat resemble, except for the gorgeous face and muscular but graceful dancing part. I plan a lot of dances in which I just sort of stand there with my arms akimbo while other vastly more talented dancers do all the heavy lifting."

"Ballet audiences are accustomed to seeing tiny anorexic women prancing about," Mr. Spicer added. "I hope to hire no women under 250 lbs. Audiences are going to have 'Otherness' up the wazoo. It's not so much pushing the envelope as winching it. We are putting in a reinforced concrete stage. Lots of rebar."

Ballet Company spokesperson Wokie McWokester said, "Sean will bring a welcome diversity to the world of dance. Everyone agrees that Diversity is our strength. It is a known fact that somewhere in the vicinity of 97 percent of straight white men can't dance. This will celebrate and validate the much-ballyhooed Other. In this case, the Other being big, clumsy straight white men who cannot dance. We are incredibly proud. We don't care if season ticket sales plunge. We stand with the Lady Ghostbusters in putting Diversity before profits. Or even Quality."

#2

GQ (formerly Gentleman's Quarterly) has announced that Jerry Nadler has been named Style Editor with a salary and benefits package of $80,000 a month. GQ Editor-in-Chief Will Welch said: "The new look for 2020 will be that belted-under-the-armpits look made so popular by Mr. Nadler, or as we call him Natty 'Nads. What a trendsetter! Although this will probably represent a cut in pay for any politician, he has agreed to step in to save the magazine from what some feared was a turn away from its legendary macho look, especially with the spring magazine showing a lot of man purses and little matching gloves. The Nadler New Direction – the baggy suit, the shirt damp with House Judicial Committee Hearing flopsweat, the food-stained tie, and especially the belt – well, he's just got it all."

#3

Jussie Smollett has been offered $80,000 a month for his scriptwriting expertise on a new whodunnit television series tentatively called "So You Want To Be A Hate Crime Victim?"

In the first storyboarding conference with the other writers Mr. Smollett emerged whimpering and visibly shaken from the raucous laughter behind the door when he insisted that a gay black man would TOTALLY go out for a Subway sandwich at 2 a.m. in Chicago in January. "Whoa, dude," said one writer, "Crack, maybe, I think we could sell that; cigarettes for sure, but a SANDWICH? What else ya got?"

"Ok, two white dudes carrying rope and bleach in an uptown neighborhood in Chicago, see this gay black guy and throw a noose around his neck and…"

"DUDE! How they know he gay?"

"The guy is FAMOUS! They watch the show he's on…"

"Two racist, homophobic old white dudes watch his show?"

"Yes."

"So, if they're fans, why would they want to hurt him? Maybe they just want his autograph?"

"But, where's the victimization in THAT? NO, they definitely put a noose around his neck."

"And, the guy doesn't fight back? Doesn't even drop his sandwich OR his cellphone? What are you saying, man? That gay black men are pansies? My gay black SISTER could open a major can of whoop-ass on two white guys who tried to put a noose around her neck."

"Don't forget the bleach! The racist MAGA guys throw bleach, too! It's very hurtful!"

"Nobody gonna believe that, dude. Nobody but Cory, Kamala, and Robin Roberts. Your own Mama will not believe two guys are just roaming around in below zero weather on spec with bleach and a rope and nobody notices. Hell, the bleach would probably freeze. How 'bout we work on a plot where five or six masked white Antifa guys with bike locks work over an elderly black man in a MAGA hat?"

"But, but, but…How is THAT a Hate Crime?"

#4

With the Resistance getting ever more vicious and aggressive, the urgent need for a Body Double for our beautiful First Lady, Melania Trump, has become obvious. Some expressed surprise when Friday Power Line guest columnist Susan "Ammo Grrrll" Vass won the coveted but dangerous job. Despite being a foot shorter and 24 years older than the First Lady as well as being utterly incapable of walking in high heels, judges proclaimed her a dead ringer for Melania after she beat the younger, taller ladies in the critical return-fire portion of the interview.

"The $80,000 a month will come in handy," said Mrs. Vass, "but it's the opportunity to 'take one for the team' that really excited me." Interviewed on the Fox And Friends morning show, the hosts touched on a possible flaw in the plan. "No offense, Mrs. Vass," Pete Hegseth asked, "but isn't the First Lady kind of statuesque, where as YOU are…uh, not?"

"Well, it all depends on what 'statue' you refer to. I am several inches taller than the average garden gnome, for example."

Mrs. Vass plans to make an appearance as Body Double on The View where they have requested a display of her shooting skills.

"I plan to shoot a fruit off the head of Joy Behar; nothing so large as an apple, probably a grape. I'll be using my Sig Sauer .45 or, as The View brainiacs described it in the promo piece for the show, my 'fully-automatic assault weapon that I got through the gun show loophole.' Gosh, I hope I don't get too nervous being on television or too wobbly trying to wear Melania-style spike heels."

WHAT YOU NEED GOING FORWARD

DECEMBER 13. 2019

I confess. Though it's supposed to be bad manners, I love to eavesdrop. Since I often travel alone, it is not unusual to find myself in situations where I am just sitting there in a restaurant at my pathetic Table For One, pretending to study the menu. All around me various conversations are swirling that give me some idea of what my fellow countrymen are thinking. (Or did, before whole families just hunkered over their individual cellphones.)

Perhaps the conversation that delighted me the most – that can still make me laugh aloud when I relive it – took place in one of those big, heavily advertised roadside souvenir shops that dot the landscape from Arizona through Texas. I was actually an aisle away from the family, but I heard a youngster's voice. He had grabbed an item off a shelf, determined to have it for his own. "But, WHY can't I have it? I NEED IT! I NEED IT!" he asserted loudly and tearfully, working his way up to a major meltdown. And this is what I heard:

"No, Cody! Put that back! No 5 year old NEEDS a bullwhip." Surely, truer words were never spoken. "Need" is such a relative term, isn't it? (Gun show t-shirt: "Why, yes, I DO have all the guns that I NEED; but, I don't have all the guns that I WANT.")

Politically, it's going to be a long, hard slog for eleven months until we can reelect Donald Trump. We are going to need a lot of morale boosting in a fight in which all the might, all the power are seemingly arrayed against us. Who is still on our side – besides the 63 million Clinging Deplorables who elected him? It gets gosh-darn discouraging. And every day seems to feature a new defector, usually taking a gratuitous potshot at US on his way out the door.

Here is a partial list of those NOT on our side: the powerful gatekeepers of social media; most mainline church hierarchies; The Bloated Deep State; almost every billionaire; the Arrogant Academic Slugs; the Millionaire Athletes on their Plantations; Every Major Network including much of Fox; The Mewling Pussy Hat Crowd; The First Amendment Haters; The Gun Grabbers; the Incredibly Diverse Identicrats; the Prevaricating Pollsters; the Late-Night Commie-dians; and the Spineless Entertainment Industry Twits, if they want to work.

(Hollywood's Motto: "Let's remake every movie ever made, only this time in *Die Hard*, the Bruce Willis character is a lesbian Mexican dwarf who kicks Trump off the Nakatomi Tower!" I hear that Hollywood is working on an *ET* remake with Elliot all grown up having a reunion with ET. Perfect. If we get to meet ET's extended family, Adam Schiff could play his deranged older brother who is insanely jealous because ET is cuter with a much shorter neck.)

Perhaps most discouraging of all are the miserable turncoats, petty snipers, and Professional Pretend Republicans in print and on TV. Look, Ana "Fat!" Navarro, I don't care if you are now all-in for gun-grabbing, baby-killing, border-erasing, Medicare for illegals. There's a Party for that. Just OWN IT. Tell the world proudly that you are now a Democrat. And that goes for the whole tiresome Never Trump outfit as well. Take a page from the gutsy gays and just come out, already.

My take is that damn few of the turncoats have a military background, nor have most even ever been in a bar fight. Why do I say this? Because if they had been in a real down and dirty fight with a relentless, implacable enemy, they would know you don't snipe at your teammates over some utter triviality when they are all that stands between you and disaster.

("Hey, did you hear that the President's salt shaker was bigger than the others on the table? Seriously, you guys. He got more ice cream once, too, and his wife wore high heels to a hurricane! Plus, her Christmas decorations are icky, that's what all the cool people said.")

Though this is a deadly serious fight, we are going to need humor, stamina, endurance, and constant reminders of why we fight. The Loony Left will supply the latter. And here is where I think I can help. My newest column compilation book – *Ammo Grrrll Is A Straight Shooter* – is now out on Amazon and available for purchase in bulk for the holidays. I promise it will be a morale-builder, a load-lightener, and fun stroll back down a pretty recent Memory Lane.

I love recommending other people's work (good comics, musicians, and my husband, Max Cossack's excellent novels). I do not like pushing my own stuff. Frankly, I never even mentioned Book Four — *Ammo Grrrll Is Home On The Range* — but it also covers a fun period of recent history in which the Left has behaved with all the decorum of a kindergarten class that missed its nap on the day after ingesting 80 lbs. of Halloween candy. Feel free to order both books if you missed Book Four. Please. I thank you in advance. If just a couple hundred fans buy the new book, it will vault it to #1 in Political Humor on Amazon! Then give it a 5-Star Review! It really really helps.

"For every single 5-Star Review, a drop is drained from the DC Slough!" – Clarence the Angel in "It's a Wonderful Life." You can look it up.

All 5 books, which I have put out in just 13 months, sport vibrant, pretty covers. So if you are one of those people who just like to display books rather than read them, they will make an attractive addition to any bookshelf. Since each individual column takes but 5-8 minutes to read, you can see how perfect the book would be for the bathroom. They are also good for bedtime reading before you crash. Which, in my case, is usually about 6 minutes. At this rate I hope to finish *Green Eggs and Ham* by New Year's Day.

I won't be doing another self-promotion for at least 5 months when *Ammo Grrrll Reloads* (Volume 6) comes out. It will cover April 2019 through March 2020. After that, I will be – Whew! – caught up and will only put out one a year. That's one column of self-promotion out of 52. Not bad, really, for a person who toils for free! If you've ever listened to a Rush hour, you get 5 minutes of Rush, 5 minutes of commercials; lather, rinse, repeat. It's OKAY. For the incalculable contributions Rush has made to the cause, he's entitled!

May your Christmas or Chanukah be joyous; renew, refresh, and saddle up for the coming battle. Let my work be a burr under the saddle of our opponents, and a balm to your soul.

THE NO POPPYCOCK TOUR

December 20, 2019

Though the behavior of the denizens of the Democrat Klown Kar and the entire wretched Party pretty much defies parody, periodically I like to give it my best shot. You couldn't possibly make up that A.C. Green said we must impeach President Trump either because he is going to win or because of slavery, take your pick. Soooo…

Inspired by the No Malarkey Tour, I have decided to throw my hat into the ring in Iowa in the Democrat Primary with the No Poppycock Tour. Heck – I enjoy traveling, shaking hands, kissing babies, biting fingers and smelling hair as much as the next person, as long as the next person is Joe "Nothing Weird To See Here" Biden. (Memo to self: Do NOT bite the babies and smell people's fingers ever again. Bad optics all round! For sure, never SHAKE the babies or bite ladies' hair. So much to learn and do right! How DOES Joe do it? Harder than it looks!)

Q & A from my first meet-the-candidate open forum in Des Moines:

Q: Pudgy audience member: Two questions: Is it true that you used your massive influence as a regular weekly customer to ask the owner of a fancy jazz club in St. Paul to employ your son as a busboy? And do you think you are too old for such a vigorous campaign?

A: Hey, Fat, if anything, my son was OVERQUALIFIED for that busboy job. He had just earned a college degree in English! He spoke English very goodly and also a little French, in case somebody from Montreal needed to find the bathroom. Or the library. He could carry dirty dishes with the best of them, by cracky. I suggested $80,000 a month, and the club owner countered with “minimum wage plus tips” and he prevailed. Doh! There was no quid pro quo, none! My husband and I enjoyed going there to drink and watch our son work.

Boy, the idea that I am too old just frosts my cupcake! How old are you, Tubby? Wanna have a race to the cookies over there, huh? You’re a daisy if you do! Wanna do some yoga? Let’s see you do the Salute to the Sun or Downward Facing Dog. Were YOU #1 in your high school class? I am not too old, bub, and I plan to speak to that guy Allen, Adam, Aaron, some A-word Schiff who is gonna find your phone records – or somebody’s phone records – and put them in a report. How do you like them apples?

So, who’s your huckleberry now, Chubby? Where’d you get your talking points – from Putin? I bet you know Tulsi Gabbard who some bitter alcoholic loser sussed out is a Russian asset. She’s cute, though, and her hair smells like coconut…What was the question again?

Q: Woman in a crewcut: Miz Vass, do you have an opinion on gay marriage?

A: I do. Next question?

Q: Same woman wrestling the mic back from the moderator: Uh…might we know what that position is?

A: Listen, Fatso, I agree with President Barack Hussein Obama that marriage is a thing between one man and one woman, unless you are a Democrat from Katie Hill’s district in California and then it’s either three or one and a dog. I am not a racist, so I could not possibly disagree with anything Obama says. I have a souvenir plaque I got in Texas that says “Marriage is an endless sleepover with your favorite weirdo.” And then I saw one in a little diner in Iowa that said, “Marriage: you start out with two hearts and a diamond and end up wanting a club and a spade." What do you think about that, because my husband, the famous novelist Max Cossack, did not think it was as humorous as I did?

Q: Same woman: First of all, I am a personal trainer and I weigh 115 lbs., so I do not understand why you have called me Fatso, especially when you could stand to drop twenty pounds yourself. But you never answered the question.

A: Did too, Thunder Thighs. The Russian "women" always did very well in the Olympics, especially the ones wearing athletic cups. I'm beginning to think with all these Putin talking points that you might be a Russian asset, comrade, or even a Russian. Next question!

Q: Soldier in camo fatigues: I also have a two part question. First, what are you going to do for our vets? And second, how many more years should we stay in Afghanistan?

A: Listen, son, I take a back seat to no one on support for the awesome men and women who neuter our pets. When we lost our cat, Tiger…[breaks down in tears and then recovers]…our vet actually sent us a special sympathy card and it meant the world to us.

Q: Ma'am. Sorry about your cat, but I am not a veterinarian. I am in the U.S. Army.

A: Oh, haha. That's one on me. I thought you were going hunting later. I know what it's like to be in combat. I have been a standup at the Mickey Finn's comedy club in the basement of the Union Hall. What's the difference between being heckled and having an RPG fired at you? None. Words are exactly as hurtful. Ask any misgendered lunatic. True, there aren't Veterans Hospitals filled with people who had "You suck" or "Ma'am" hurled at them, but it still leaves scars, believe you me!

Q: Ma'am, if I might repeat the question, how long on Afghanistan?

A: Oh, yeah. I wish Afghanistan was spelled Efghinistan, because then there would be 5 letters – efghi – in a row from the alphabet in the same word, instead of just three (fgh) — how cool would THAT be?

I think if a baby is born and graduates from high school and we're still in the same war, that war is a little long. But, it's important to keep up with the Europeans. Now THERE'S some folks who can prolong a war. The Thirty Years' War? Fuggidaboudit. The Hundred Years' War? So, if we want to be more like Europe, we've got a ways to go. Also on wait times to see a doctor. We lag way behind on that. Sometimes people can even be seen the same day here. I personally know a woman who went in with a painful hip and had that hip replaced the next day! Don't like going to the doctor? Vote for me and my fellow Democrats, and you may never see one again! And that's no poppycock. Say, is that doughnuts over there? With sprinkles?

MIDWAY! DO NOT MISS IT!

December 27, 2019

I really do not go to movies in a theater. We are appalled by most of the braindead twits in Hollywood and do not care to help pay for their relentless attacks on everything we value – America, masculine male men, the military, cops, fossil fuels, Christianity, observant Judaism, the rule of law, capitalism, free speech, secure borders, Israel, and the like.

But when two of your best friends invite you to go to dinner and a movie, you don't want to come off as a fanatical jerk, either. Especially when the movie in question was *Midway*. I did not look at any of the reviews before going. It does not matter to me what some hipster Intersectional Studies major a third my age thinks about anything. My husband, the novelist Max Cossack, did point out before we went that the Reviewers as an aggregate had given it a pathetic 42% favorable rating, while the audiences had given it a 92% favorable rating!

Now since I have seen it, I skimmed a few of the predictable reviews. One of the most enraging to me, written by some lame-o whose name does not matter, claims that "there was no one in particular to root for!" That speaks volumes. How 'bout AMERICA, fool?

Yes, not only did the American good guys have the temerity to win, but there was not a single scrawny woman superhero using her tiny fists to dispatch someone the size of The Rock. Oh, there were heroic women aplenty besides the tireless medical personnel. The heroic women were the brave wives of the sailors and airmen who kept the home fires burning, waiting for their men to survive every mission, praying for miracles, and bearing loss with dignity and pride. As the granddaughter of a Gold Star Mother, I know something of the life-altering cost of that kind of sacrifice.

For my entire life, of course, I had heard about the cowardly and devastating attack on Pearl Harbor. When you're a kid, you picture some planes fly over, sink some ships and glug, glug, glug, down they go. That actual humans were involved does not register. Yes, I realize that was hopelessly naive. In *Midway*, the Pearl Harbor attack was relentless and horrific, though the movie mostly shows us that through heartbreaking small details rather than gore.

The movie failed to sugarcoat the Pearl Harbor attack, the Battle of Midway, and the egregious war crimes of the Japanese. Certainly in the modern era, I had never seen that emphasized before. All Americans were supposed to feel immense guilt over Hiroshima; that was the only "atrocity" one could mention aloud. Never mind that it probably saved a million American lives had a landed invasion of Japan been necessary, and a great many Japanese lives as well, conceivably many times what were lost from the atomic bombs.

You can see why the left-leaning reviewers would give this movie only one or two stars out of five. In the movie, great toxic male heroism is not only on constant display, but the dreaded American INDIVIDUALISM as well. Individual effort not only mattered; it was decisive.

Oddly for a modern movie, with one exception definitely in context, there were no f-bombs, and no subplots with gratuitous sex and nudity. Whether that is a positive or negative is up to you, but once the Battle of Midway commenced, this audience member felt like she was in peril every harrowing minute and sex was not much on my mind. Truth to tell, what transpired, what those incredible patriots did, was really almost impossible to absorb.

For some deep background on the Battle of Midway, I turned to my friend, Tony — that's Ernest F. "Tony" Peluso, Lieutenant Colonel, United States Army (Ret.) to most — or as the commenter family knows him — TonyP173. He was kind enough to share many edifying thoughts with us. I will put his words in quotes lest anyone mistakenly believe that I am any kind of authority on this subject.

"The Battle of Midway was, in my opinion, the decisive battle of the whole war, and the high water mark for the Japanese Empire. The fact that the dive bombers were able to take out the first three carriers was a total fluke. Until that time, the Japanese were beating the holy hell out of us, and we hadn't laid a glove on them. After Midway, and because of our singular industrial potential, the Japanese could not compete in replacing the lost carriers, and went on the defensive.

"Less well considered is how Midway affected the war in Europe. Had we LOST the Battle of Midway, the Japanese would most certainly have invaded Hawaii. Though we now know that they had no plans to invade the continental USA, they had already taken islands in the Aleutian Chain. So they could have easily threatened the USA, raided, and harassed. I don't see how FDR could have sold a Germany first policy if the West Coast were threatened. As a result, and because we were woefully unprepared to fight WWII, we could NOT have sent the 8th Air Force to England to begin the daylight precision bombing. A little known sad fact: there were more KIAs in the 8th Air Force in WWII, than in the entire USMC in the Pacific, which in no way minimizes those great sacrifices, of course, but gives us some perspective.

"Without the early sacrifices in blood and material, which inhibited the development of super weapons (like jet aircraft and V1/V2 rockets, let alone an atom bomb), there could have been no invasion of North Africa, let alone France. This means that Hitler could have fielded jet aircraft in large numbers by late 1943, and that would have changed things enormously. He could have begun building V2s in large numbers, and — unconcerned by a possible second front in the west — could have dealt far more effectively with the Russians.

"So, it's plausible that the Allies could have lost the war with Germany (or been unable to beat Germany decisively) because America had to focus its resources on Japan first. This is not far-fetched. As you know, I think everything happens for a reason, and the Midway victory is one of those miracles that change history."

Thanks so much, Tony. Anyway, the movie is great. I know this hasn't been a laugh riot of a column, but sometimes, we must speak of more serious things to remind ourselves of the legacy we inherited and its price tag. *Midway* really is the kind of movie that should be seen in a theater, but heck, most flatscreen TVs nowadays are roughly the size of movie screens. So even if it leaves the theaters, do not miss it. Woody Harrelson does a particularly good job as Admiral Nimitz. My Uncle Leland (USMC) gave his life in the Pacific and his nephew, my brother, served on the aircraft carrier Nimitz in the Mediterranean.

JANUARY THRU MARCH 2020

The great cosmic odometer turns over to 2020, which numbers have been associated forever with clarity of vision. Oh boy. Since I am finishing up this book a whole year later with perfect hindsight, I just say, "Thank God we don't know what is coming next or we might all do the old Thelma and Louise dead run into the Grand Canyon." But, for the nonce, let's pretend we don't know what's in store in 2020, okay?

The columns in January feature discussions on the crime of "dead-naming", on the benefits of claiming perpetual and eternal victim status, and a column on "People I Have Been Happiest to See in My Life." Also, a launch of Max Cossack's fourth novel, Low Tech Killers. Max has a tough time trying to write parody of the Wokesters, since they are all in a race to the bottom to out-woke and cancel each other. But the book is a fun romp.

February includes a passionate tribute to my favorite Ruger shirt, a report card of low marks for the Super Bowl ads, a realistic look at Geriatric Multi-Tasking, and a little good-natured sniping at the media.

March starts off with a column about the Oscars and then, as Life takes a tumble into the absurd, the dangerous, and the periodically terrifying, a new loose virus quickly becomes a world-wide pandemic. The last three columns in March all concern prepping for the 2-week voluntary lockdown to "flatten the curve".

It's possible that nothing in our lives will never be the same again. But, we don't know that yet. So, just relax and enjoy the read and the ride.

The final column in this book, "Ammo Grrrll Reloads" is a

celebration of the column turning six!

JENNIFER RUBIN: ARROGANT SNOB FOR THE AGES

January 3, 2020

Remember when the Khmer Rouge under mass murderer Pol Pot killed everyone in Cambodia with glasses or – if they were lucky – just exiled them from the city to be worked to death on farms? Yeah, that was awesome. People with glasses might have been educated and that was, you know, "elitist" and bad. God forbid, they were just normal yokels with poor vision, but oh well, when making those tasty Commie Omelets, you gotta break a few eggs. By incomplete records, around 2-3 million broken eggs…in Cambodia alone.

Now we see Twitter Queen, Fake Republican and Miserable, Haggard Old Berkeley grad and Trump Hater Jennifer Rubin chiming in on somebody else's Tweet that the Trump Party will soon be a "rump party" of Southern crackers who don't talk goodly like the elite does. And Jenny adds: "and non-college educated." Jenny, you ignorant hack, you say that like it's a BAD thing. Sort of a reverse image of Pol Pot, not yet as dangerous, but plenty bigoted — this time out, the working stiffs are anathema instead of the educated. Am I saying Jennifer Rubin is a mass murderer? Of course not. Grow up. But a snotty snob for sure.

Okay, just for the record, almost every Trump supporter that I know PERSONALLY, has not just a college degree, but advanced and multiple degrees, so it's a lie on the face of it, but the outrageous arrogance that would make Rubin say such a thing is what I find most disturbing. It's of a piece with our dear friends in the unbiased, neutral media saying we are "smelly" Walmart shoppers with bad teeth.

How hard is it to be a college graduate anyway? I just remembered that even I went to college – three of them in fact over an 18-year period – and eventually earned a Speech Communication Degree from a fourth-rate diploma factory. That citadel of scholarship has morphed in the last couple of decades into a motley morass of microaggression sleuths ferreting out Deplorable "ists" hither and yon. The last time I darkened its doorstep, there were actually little signs on the desks in Administration that said, "This is a violence-free workplace." I burst out laughing. "Well, I guess that distinguishes it from all the other workplaces that welcome and encourage violence," I said to my tour guide who did not quite know what to say. Especially since I was at that time a member of the Board of Trustees, and generous donor. In Academia, disagreement IS "violence." Sad. So sad.

But back to Sweet Jenny. Can you dear readers even THINK of anything more Untouchable than a non college-educated person? Icky-poo! Let me list a couple college-free people it has been my honor to know whose native intelligence – not even to mention USEFULNESS – has got to be greater than Jenny's by several orders of magnitude. Unlike Cornpop, Warren's Cherokee MeeMaw or Corey Booker's pseudonymous friend, these are real people:

Elaine. She is the widow of my father's lifelong friend in Bryant, South Dakota. A very prosperous farm woman, she sewed all her own clothes, even making her own patterns. She is a country cook whose food would make hipster chefs weep with envy, bakes elaborate wedding cakes as a sideline business, tended a half-acre vegetable garden well into her 80s, makes quilts, knits, crochets, and can do all manner of needlework. Naturally, she canned all her own garden produce. There is no farm task which she couldn't do alongside her late husband. Alas, no college degree and, it goes without saying, a Trump Republican.

Enrique: He may or may not be a Trump supporter, but it really doesn't matter because he is a Jehovah's Witness who does not vote. The fact that he is also an illegal would normally be no barrier to his voting because he now lives in California. I just want to honor him as one of the smartest non college-educated people I have ever met, and someone with whom I would rather spend all day any day than one minute with Jennifer Rubin.

The fourth of 10 children born to a single mother in Southern Mexico, Enrique only got to go to school to about the 5th grade, and then sporadically. He was needed to bring in money to the desperately poor family. From the time he was a toddler he shined shoes, picked up cans, and did any odd job that anyone would give him a peso for. Sometimes his mother would send him on kind of a Trick-or-Treat journey to the neighbors to beg for "a couple of tortillas just for the younger kids." The older ones went hungry.

By middle school age, he apprenticed himself to a variety of older workingmen to learn car mechanics, carpentry, plumbing, electrical work, and any other skill anyone would teach him. After he came to the U.S., he learned professional window-washing and, of course, landscaping. He loved all plants and sang to them or whistled while he worked. It was a point of pride to him that he never went to the fields, though he had nothing but respect for those who did. He was married, with a severely mentally challenged daughter, but you would think he was the happiest man in the world. He worked for me for five years. It was uplifting just to be around him and I cried for days when he moved.

Lest the list go on indefinitely, let me just assure Ms. Snotty Pants that almost everything she eats, everything that gets delivered by semis from one place to another and Amazon, every item of clothing she wears, every drop of fuel she pumps, every piece of ore from the ground, the assembly of every car she drives (or is driven in), the construction of her home(s) and the printing of every book she has ever read, was PROBABLY provided by hard-working people who never went to college. Maybe some of them did and good for them! Even family farming has gotten complicated enough that a college education is helpful, if not absolutely necessary.

At least in the olden days, if you majored in Agriculture, you would probably be studying subjects critical to, uh, Farm Stuff, and not a lot of postmodern deconstruction of English Literature. (Hint: If you DO have to take such a course, just babble on tediously about sexism, imperialism, and white and male supremacy until everything uplifting, creative, universal and original is leached out of the work of art, and you'll be fine…) I'm pretty sure that Mining and Mineral Extraction requires a big team of people with advanced knowledge in Sciencey things like Geology and various forms of Engineering that I know nothing about. But there is still going to be an army of roughnecks and big guys doing dirty jobs to make the thing work.

See, Jen, there's a REASON that talking heads on television were never asked to become part of an industrial union. It's because no one would miss them if they went on strike. Give it a whirl and see how long it takes for the Great Unwashed Without College to agree to give up Trump if only you will, pretty please, come back and brighten their lives. Finally, is it just me, or do these deranged Trump Haters actually age faster than normal? I guess being that miserable, furious, and ungrateful takes its toll on both mind and body.

THREE EVENTS I WILL BE MISSING IN 2020 AND BEYOND

January 10, 2020

Well, 2020 has started off with a literal BANG with the surprising vaporization of Revered, Austere, Terrorist Psychopath and Poetry Lover, "Casey" Qassem Soleimani. The Democrat politicians, celebrities, and media slugs are slowly working their way through the Five Stages of Grief. So far there has been no funeral stampede by distraught Democrats with 40 of them being crushed underfoot, but it's only a matter of time. A few days later, there was a full frontal assault on the Hollywood attention junkies by Ricky Gervais at the Golden Globe Awards. The only way that Ricky could have been more brutal was if he had had a Gatling gun.

So what can we expect in the way of Must-See Events in 2020? Well, here are the Top Three which your humble columnist will be missing.

THE TAKE AN ENTITLED, UNPLEASANT, RACIST BLACK WOMAN TO DINNER EVENT

Yeah, that's a thing now. It's called "Race to Dinner." According to an article in the Daily Caller, a black woman named Regina Jackson is organizing dinners for white women to attend with women of some color other than white. Oh, this will not entail a few laughs and sharing recipes, kid pix, or discussing what all lucky American women have in common. Heaven forfend! No. White women who are masochists without a shred of dignity, can sign up to listen all evening to how complicit they are with white supremacy because of the color of their skin. They can't even talk! They are there simply to "bear witness to the pain of black and brown women," pain which…wait for it… white women have caused. What a crock!

Yeah, I'll be missing that. Sure, it sounds fun, but I have never been one to sit quietly and take a lot of ludicrous and insulting guff. The only thing more repulsive would be to have to hear that tedious tirade from Kirsten Gillibrand, or AOC, or Elizabeth Warren, three women whose actual "color" is white as the driven snow.

The Daily Caller gives us a little background on Ms. Jackson, explaining that she "grew up in Chicago during the time of the Martin Luther King slaying." She also makes a glancing reference to the 1964 murders of "Goodman, Chaney, and Schwerner" in Mississippi.

Odd she should mention these two events, which occurred more than half a century ago. First of all, in the grotesque Mississippi murders, Goodman and Schwerner were Jews, WHITE martyrs giving their lives for civil rights. In fact, of all white Freedom Riders in the Civil Rights Era, fully 75 percent of those idealistic young people were Jewish!

Second, on April 4, 1968, the very day MLK was slain, what this white girl was doing was hosting a wedding reception for a white bride and a black groom in Chicago. Neither set of parents approved or would attend, so the couple – with a little three-month-old baby already here — got married in our tiny 4th floor walkup apartment. I baked the cake and other refreshments. They even used our own wedding bands to exchange vows. The small guest list was pretty evenly divided between white and black people, and, since the King murder had just happened, you could have cut the tension in the room with a knife. As the night wore on amid reports of the inevitable, pointless arson and looting on the South and West Side, the party ended and the groom took off so he could help calm things down in his old neighborhood. I minded the baby and got the frantic new bride involved in baking bread to distract her. You know, like any old white supremacist would. I mean, it was WHITE BREAD, you guys! It was 52 years ago, so I can't remember if I made the OK sign too.

THE ACADEMY AWARDS

I know a couple of well-connected Hollywood people who PROBABLY could score me a ticket to the Oscars if I wanted to sit way in the back and buy an outfit that cost more than my first new car. Oh, the suspense! What WILL that zany Robert De Niro say next? First, at the Tonys, he slayed the audience just with "Eff Trump," as the Trained Hollywood Seals jumped up to bark and clap their pleasure with such a clever bit of middle school repartee. The only things missing were balls to balance on the noses of the attendees. His vulgarity was such a hit, he said it again! Whoa! "Eff Trump!" But that just wasn't enough. Apparently, the repulsive little geezer hadn't had any attention for a few months, and he recently Tweeted that the President deserved something yet more humiliating. He advised that someone should "throw s*** in Trump's face." Classy. Especially from a wart-faced little old man wearing 6 inch lift shoes. He personally couldn't even REACH Trump's face without a step stool.

Let me tell you something, Bobby Boy: nobody despised Barack Hussein Obama more than I did, but he WAS #MyPresident for 8 insufferable years. So when that Russian flunkie refused to shake his hand, I was enraged that the American President would get treated like that. Not only did I not wish that some mental defective would throw San Fran Sidewalk Slush in his face, but it would never even enter my head to THINK it, let alone to say it aloud. Who ARE you people? You and Madonna and Kathy Griffin and George Lopez, and all the other murder porn fantasists need to get some psychiatric help – STAT.

ANYTHING BY OR WITH MICHAEL MOORE

For about a minute and a half in 2016, Michael Moore seemed to have accidentally said a truth. The sloppy, lard-butted faux advocate for the Working Man, had predicted that Trump might win if somebody didn't start paying attention to the left-behind working class. In other words, he actually had an explanation for Hillary's loss besides rampant sexism or the Deplorability of 63 million voters. But it turned out that his assumption that maybe the working and middle-class voters had a logical reason to vote against Hillary was just a temporary brain infarction, not even as long-lasting as Eric Swalwell's, and the moment quickly passed.

Now he has gone all-in on Crazy. His latest pronouncement is that "since two of three White Men voted for Trump, if you are walking down the street and see three White Men, you should get out of the way." A statement so stupid, even on a Math and Logic level, the mind reels. Personally, if I am walking down the street and see doughy white Michael Moore, who is the poundage EQUIVALENT of 3 normal white guys, I will definitely move off the sidewalk to avoid being crushed. I guess he is divorced now, so maybe this anti-white gibberish is just to score with some Woke Chicks. I would personally recommend taking a shower and washing his hair, maybe lose the baseball cap, as a better strategy, but what do I know? Heck, I haven't had a "date" since 1967.

DEAD-NAMING: THE WORST THING THERE EVER WAS

January 17, 2020

If you live long enough, you will have the chance to hear astonishing things. Often, twice. Ideas cycle around like fashions. What was passe becomes "retro" and comes around again a couple of decades later. Hemlines go up and down. I remember when the fashion industry went to mid-calf and maxi dresses to FORCE fashionistas to purchase new clothes. When hemlines just kept going up and up to loin-cloth levels, a whole lot of young ladies, myself included, just kept cutting off and hemming up their old skirts and dresses rather than buying new garments! Or, even ROLLING them up if you were really lazy or went to Catholic Girls' School. Old becomes new again. Only the coolest people can keep up.

For example, I have learned fairly recently that "dead-naming" means calling a trans person by the name he or she was born with and used for decades! Dead-naming is a GRIEVOUS sin which will get you Twittered to death in a heartbeat, and possibly sent to jail in Canada or in the U.S. if a Democrat ever gets in again, God forbid! So though we cheered him and honored him and put him on Wheaties boxes long ago, Bruce Jenner and all his accomplishments may never again be mentioned. Bruce Jenner is dead. Long live Caitlyn.

I try to call people what they want to be called. In real life (a place a lot of leftists rarely visit…), my name is Susan. My Daddy and a very small circle of my friends have always called me Susie, and that's fine. In the last eight years, I have been called and will answer to "Ammo Grrrll" or even "AG." Both my husband and Mama always called me Susan and that is what I was mostly called in high school. Nowadays, few married women take their husbands' names. It makes addressing holiday cards a pain, but on the other hand, it sure makes finding your old female friends a lot easier. So though I have had my husband's last name for 52 years, I would not pitch a hysterical fit if someone called me by my "dead" or "maiden" name! Because I am not insane.

Anybody know what the deal is with gay men and the formality they seem to prefer in names? Maybe your experience is different, but every gay man I have ever known – and remember, I lived in San Francisco just off Castro Street for several years – wanted to be called Robert, or Michael, or James. Never Bobby, Mike or Jimmy. A notable exception would be Pete Buttigieg. Though, I suppose if you are a gay man and Butt is already part of your name, adding Peter to the mix would be a bridge too far.

Here's the thing, see. I'm sure there are still a few hardcore homophobes (a very stupid, inaccurate word, but what passes for "someone who is put off by or hostile to gay people"). But there are also very few people who don't have a friend, a cousin, a sibling, a workmate who is, in fact, gay. And often it was observed that some of those people had stable, loving, long-term partners. Meanwhile, your heterosexual nephew's marriage blew up before your check cleared for the set of sixteen silver shrimp forks you were forced to purchase from their Gift Registry because all the cheap stuff had already been taken.

You don't have to be some kind of bigot to have had or continue to have serious concerns about the long-term effects to civilization of changing the millennia-old definition of "marriage." Things that have been absolutely foundational to society should not be abandoned lightly. At the same time, you can also be a fair-minded person who thinks that Daniel and

Kevin next door, who have been together for 28 years, deserve some kind of recognition of that relationship and some legal protection in the matter of hospital visits or inheritance.

But it's academic anyway because that battle was lost. A massive societal alteration was decided by a total of five Americans – FIVE! — after being soundly defeated for the second time by California referendum, even in the Obama tsunami of 2008. And did the losers riot in the street, carry a beheaded image of Obama around, start fires, attack police or even (God forbid) physically attack gay people? No, they did not. Compare and contrast with what happened after the 2016 election when 63 MILLION voters and a yuge majority of the Electoral College upset the predetermined coronation of Hillary Clinton.

You know who committed virtual and actual violence after gay marriage won? THE WINNERS. Winning was not enough. People – well, not Obama, of course – but people, who a few years earlier had supported traditional marriage, were "outed," fired and "canceled."

And quicker than you could get used to calling Kevin's partner Daniel his "husband" or, worse, his "wife." another country was heard from. Yes! In the Diversity Olympics, ding, ding, ding, we now have a new Top Dog Winner: The Transgenders!! Move over, you boring old gay people, who are happy with your sex and attracted to others of that same sex! In the Brave New World of Intersectional Politics, that will no longer be allowed. Lesbians – you will now be required to date men with dangly bits who are wearing dresses and have decided that they are now women. Only attracted to real women? Tough noogies, bigot!

Woe unto the poor young salesclerk in a hardware store who "misgenders" an ugly, rude, clearly unhinged giant of a man who feels entitled to kick over merchandise in a store because he has accurately been called "Sir" instead of

"Ma'am." (As a woman with a fairly deep speaking voice, many is the time I have been called "Sir" on the telephone when making a plane or hotel reservation. Had I known I could pitch a hysterical fit or get someone fired because of it, think of the 15 minutes of fame I could have by now! Maybe even cash money!)

Which brings us full circle back to the dead-naming. Because to support the massive illusion of sex being just a fluid construct requires a Stalinist devotion to erasing everything that has gone before. It is of a piece, really, with the Taliban dynamiting Buddhist statuary, pretend "Palestinians" like Egyptians Yassir Arafat or Edward Said, claiming that Jews were never in Israel, and with the history haters tearing down Confederate statues.

In totalitarian circles, inconvenient history and unacceptable ideas that are declared Dead must never be resurrected. Likewise, if you say you are a woman now, then you must always have been a woman and woe be unto some Un-wokester who mentions your past. I can sympathize because I used to be a leftist. I wish I could pretend it never happened, but I am more honest than that. I have friends who have been married multiple times; they have made peace with dead relationships and moved on. But, especially if there are children involved, they do not punish anyone who remembers they used to be married to someone else. Or even several someone elses. Because they are not insane.

We have entered a whole 'nother surreal realm of Crazy. Nothing good can come of it.

YOU ONLY SEE WHAT YOU'RE LOOKING FOR

January 24, 2020

A couple of weeks ago, I was planning a small, informal dinner party which would include an awesome lemon pie. I bought whipping cream in lieu of making meringue. One of my Guiding Life Principles is that there are few foods which are not improved by the addition of either whipped or sour cream. If there is leftover whipped cream, I like to top off my coffee with it as a special treat. So I bought two containers.

Fast forward to the day of the party. I open the fridge and look for the containers of cream. Where are the squatty little pink and white cardboard cartons? Nowhere in sight. What the heck, or words to that effect? Oh, maybe I put them in the "beverage fridge" in the laundry room? Nope. Try the kitchen fridge again, moving some things around, looking behind the 20 yogurts and depressing Rubbermaid containers of leftovers not getting any younger. Nope. Back to the laundry room…at least I'm getting some extra steps on my pedometer.

This went on four more times, until I employed the old Sherlock Holmes logic: "Once you eliminate the impossible, whatever remains, no matter how improbable, must be the truth."

I knew the following to be true: I had bought two containers of Heavy Whipping Cream. I refrigerated them. Therefore, they MUST be there. And to my shock and delight: there they were! In plain sight! But here's the kicker – they were NOT the small squatty pink and white cardboard cartons; they were taller green and white plastic bottles. Which I eventually recalled I had chosen because they were bigger with a later "Best by" date.

My eye had skipped right over them. I could not "see" them because they were not what I was looking for. Whoa! And stumbled upon an important truth about us: we often only see what we are looking for, not what is right in front of us. (Move over, Marianne Williamson…here comes Ammo Grrrll, the Accidental Philosopher).

I thought about all the lonely women I had known who had really kind, smart, average-looking guys who clearly liked them, but they had their eyes on either rich guys or "hotties" who wouldn't give them the time of day. They chose loneliness over companionship with someone who didn't meet their superficial standards. Men, too, are kind of famous for that; it is a theme of at least 90 percent of romantic movies, including such classics as *When Harry Met Sally*. (Though one would have to wonder about the romantic discernment of a fella who has Meg Flippin' Ryan right there and can't see it…oh well, to each his or her own.)

Let me give you another example, even more important. Long ago, I had read a nice little parable about a river ferry operator who took Northerners and Southerners back and forth near the Mason Dixon Line. One lady going South said, "I hear Southerners are very polite, gracious hosts and fun-loving souls." The operator said, "Yes. That's what you'll find there." When a second lady making the same trip said, "I am told that Southerners are rude, cold, clannish and uncouth," the operator said, "Yes that is what you will find there."

How true it is that we only find what we are looking for. I had been hired to speak at a women's conference in Macon, Georgia. My initial problem was learning – after I had cut a little radio spot advertising my appearance – that the town was MAY-con, NOT Ma-CON. Duh. Back to the studio. My second lesson was that no matter how much trouble I had taken with my hair and makeup and outfit, it wasn't even close to enough. Lordy, Southern women are beautiful and pulled-together! Must be something in Sweet Tea.

But the most important, most shocking lesson – and this was way back in the mid-'80s – was how much more friendly and "normal" were daily relations between black and white Americans in the South than in the North. It turned out that, however wretched and sad the long history there, people seemed to approach one another as individuals much more readily. And long ago I wrote a column about going into downtown Macon, seeing two young white "rednecks" approach an elderly black man, and with my own two disbelieving eyes, seeing the young men remove their caps to chat respectfully with the gentleman for several minutes. Boy, THAT never happened in any of the Hollywood movies I had seen about the South!

And here we are in 2020, three years after a landmark election and the ever metastasizing Professional Grievance and Victim Groups refuse to admit or "see" that they are absolutely awash in liberty and opportunity. All they can see everywhere they look is racism, bigotry, and Hitler, without a shred of evidence for any of it. It is surreal. They HAVE to find oppression or lose their Special Victim Privileges. If it ISN'T hatred and bigotry that is holding them down, then they would be forced to look in the mirror and examine their life decisions. Personal responsibility is a thread that cannot be pulled on! (A sign on my desk about my fitness efforts: "Don't be upset by the results you didn't get with the work you didn't do.")

Linda Ronstadt, whose concerts I attended, whose albums I bought, has declared that not only is Trump Hitler — oh for Pete's sake, Linda, you are infringing on Joy Behar's copyrights here — but that it's "the Mexicans who are now the new Jews."

I do not expect actors and singers to be rocket scientists, especially one who has had the cartilage in her nose operated on multiple times because of perpetual cocaine use. But, that is offensive on so many levels that I can barely rebut it without my head exploding all over my keyboard. If Linda is too addled or dishonest to understand that there is a profound difference between being dragged from your soon-to-be confiscated home, put in cattle cars, and either enslaved or murdered, and sending invading freeloaders BACK to their own homes, well, then there is no hope for her, morally or intellectually.

Enough already with the stupid Hitler BS. Yeah, it's amazing how many "new Jews" we have, and yet it's still the plain old original Jews who seem never to fall off the bottom of the okay-to-hate list.

Never in human history have so many rich, pampered, cosseted people of all colors steadfastly refused to see how good they have it, or been so unwilling to defend the very system that gave them every single privilege and comfort they enjoy. They are still looking for the Magic Victim Lotto Win, even if they have to pay their own attackers, deface their own property, or put vulgar epithets on their own birthday cakes.

I think I will have another piece of lemon pie with whipped cream. It is only sexism that keeps me from my ideal weight. That, and that time 15 years ago in a private conversation where Trump said "pussy." With trauma like that to endure, who wouldn't be overweight?

PEOPLE I HAVE BEEN HAPPIEST TO SEE IN MY LIFE

January 31, 2020

There are people whom we are not at all happy to see who appear with appalling frequency – tax auditors, traffic cops when we were barely going 30 miles per hour over the posted speed suggestion, process servers, boring co-workers, freeloading distant relatives, and the like.

And then there are the sainted people who have appeared at exactly the right time and in desperate circumstances.

Although it is hard to rank such fortunate appearances, topping my list would have to be the anesthesiologist in the Labor Suite at the University of California Medical Center in San Francisco, late May 1973. Naturally, we had taken the Lamaze Class in which we learned such hilariously useless and deceitful techniques as calling a heart-stopping labor pain a "contraction," or breathing exercises destined to distract the laboring woman to the point where she hyperventilates and, mercifully, passes out temporarily.

Her husband was also supposed to be doing the heavy lifting of writing down times between "contractions," giving the wife lemon drops or ice chips for her dry mouth from all the heavy breathing, and generally telling her what a great job she was doing while removing to a safe distance anything, including JELLO, that could be used as a potential weapon.

After 17 hours of labor, repeated "dilation checks" by the nurse which was every bit as fun as it sounds, and being hooked up to a blood pressure monitor shrieking that I was near stroke level, a decision was made that it would really be best to do a C-section and soon. A lovely young man came in with fabulous drugs that deadened all the pain (I'm sorry, "contractions"), and I can honestly say that I have never before or since been happier to see an individual.

I was awake until they got the large, displeased baby out – a shockingly short time, maybe 2-3 minutes! It is a very disconcerting sensation to feel yourself being sliced open, pressure but no pain. My "coach" had been removed from the operating room lest he pass out. My doctor had appeared, with some kind of trainee in tow and the words "Don't nick the bladder, now" were mentioned, to which I heartily "seconded that emotion."

The anesthesiologist stood at my head, gently describing everything to calm me. Beautiful Baby Clone Boy was presented – Paternity Suit, Exhibit A – and then they put me under to sew me up. I had already fallen madly in love with the anesthesiologist and would happily have promised to have gratitude sex with him — although not right then — but I am pretty sure he played for the other team.

Much, much later, the first flight I was forced to take after 9/11, sometime in late October, I was flying (hate it) on a small plane (hate it), going to Montana (love it)! The entire plane was filled with hunters — large manly toxically male masculine men (my favorite kind). It was close enough to 9/11 that emotions still ran high and every man on that plane was mentally prepared to pulverize any potential terrorist with his bare hands, box cutters be damned. I was extremely happy to see them. And not just because they put my luggage into the overhead compartment and got it down again!

They were very impressed with the weapon I had snuck onto the plane in my carry-on – a baseball and a pair of tube socks. Got through Security, no problem, put the ball in the toe of the sock and tied a knot. Not as good as a Walther PPQ in 9 mm, but something to give me a fighting chance. I also had a roll of quarters as brass knuckles. (Improvise, adapt and overcome.) Thank God neither was necessary. Since there were no terrorists on the plane, I would have been just as happy to bean a femi-ninny who opened her piehole about "American Rape Culture," which subject was all the rage then and continues to this sad day.

The last Person I Was Happy To See that I will mention today – there are many more for future columns – was the Paranoid Texan shortly after we had first moved in next door to him. Sure, I had HEARD about scorpions, but had never yet seen one. My dear Mr. AG, playwright and composer, not yet novelist, had gone to San Diego to present his new play. I was not invited for the rehearsal weeks – Yoko Ono and all that. I was to join him the next day for a month in a nice condo in La Jolla. Opening a drawer to his bathroom vanity in search of a new toothbrush, there – lying among the lotions and creams – was a large ugly scorpion. I thought it was dead, but then it moved. EEEEEEEK!

I screamed and slammed the drawer, then opened it again and smushed the scorpion with whatever came to hand, if memory serves me, a deodorant. To say I was somewhat upset is to say the Democrats were mildly peeved when Donald J. Trump won the election. All I could think of was that we had to move again to a different state. I called the Paranoid Texan. He came over with a black light and searched the entire house while I hid on the patio whimpering helpfully.

Now watch this clever segue into Some Other Folks You Will Be Happy To See, albeit fictional ones. And just in time for Valentine's Day. Yes, Max Cossack has completed his fourth novel, called _Low Tech Killers_, in which we revisit his delightful cast of characters from small-town Minnesota who, oddly enough, also winter in Arizona.

You've heard of tales "ripped from today's headlines"? Max believes that gremlins (or possibly either Jeff Bezos or Putin) are stealing his fiction and turning it into reality. No sooner than he chronicles a group of Super-Woke Infighting Revolutionaries than James O'Keefe gets the goods on a brutish braindead BernieBot who can't wait to send us all to gulags. And you think the Second Amendment was some kind of afterthought the brilliant Founding Fathers just threw in to annoy future sissies and billionaire munchkin soda scolds? Anyway, I read the new novel all in one sitting because I couldn't put it down. It's hilarious and heartwarming, a cautionary tale and a blueprint for resistance.

It was said that both Napoleon and Hitler were defeated in Russia by General Mud and General Winter and once again, Minnesota winter takes a star turn in this novel. It also features an ex-father-in-law legal wizard; a precocious 10-year old trying to help her clueless father understand women; a disgraced IT guy; a moody chick singer; and, oh yeah, a great dog.

Enter the world of Hack Wilder and his long-time friend Gus Dropo, pop a beer, or pour a nice single malt Scotch, and linger over *Low Tech Killers*. Order today from Amazon. As always, Max and I thank you for your purchase and 5-Star Review on Amazon! If you are ever in the area, Max volunteers that I will cook for you. Breakfast or dinner, your choice.

RUGER SHIRT

February 7, 2020

Last Wednesday, I had a really good day at the Tactical Range. I'm sure we've all had them; you remember all your mechanics and execute well. Your weapon is really sighted in and seems to be almost incapable of missing the x-ring. You are – to use a popular sports figure of speech – IN THE ZONE. That's when it's fun. Life being what it is, there are days when you spray and pray, too. Where the harder you "try," the more tense, inaccurate and frustrated you become, like a poor hitter in a prolonged batting slump.

Afterwards I went grocery shopping, and a middle-aged produce manager at the upscale market noticed my Ruger shirt and started reminiscing about being a kid with a gun in an isolated rural area of Illinois where he was expected to protect his mother when his father was gone on trucking business. He was taught marksmanship and gun safety at age 5. By age 12, he said he could throw a tin can in the air and hit it six times before it hit the ground. In the event of a home invasion, "Participation Trophy" was not going to be good enough.

The Ruger shirt is one of my favorite garments since it is Western-style with two pockets, long sleeves and white, for protection from the Arizona sun. A Marriott Courtyard bartender in the state of Washington spotted it and told me she had a grandson named "Ruger." I asked if he had a little sister named "Kimber," and to my surprise, she got the joke. Washington may not be as far gone as feared.

The produce manager and I talked about the impressive Virginia Second Amendment rally. We agreed that the Gun Grabbers will never give up. There are different motives from several nefarious players, but the bottom line is they need a defenseless, disarmed populace to succeed. It will not happen here. Not ever. We are Americans, plain and simple. One of the few things Obama was ever right about is that we "cling" to our guns and our God, although not nearly as bitterly as his comrades cling to their hatred of President Trump. And it was a lie and a slander that we fear "Others." We recognize no "Others." We just see Americans; it is the Left that has divided us into ever smaller warring Grievance Groups.

The Gun Grabbers' first line of attack consists of bald-faced lying. They lump into the stats about "gun violence" suicides, self-defense, and accidents. Heck, I even saw a newspaper report of a funeral in Chicago which was shot up by the mourners – 12, 13 people shot – the funeral being for a career carjacker who picked the wrong car and ended up dead. The "journalist" described the late felon as "killed by gun violence." No. He was killed by stupidity, evil, and bad luck. He was ENGAGING in violence and lost. It happens.

The article was tellingly vague, but the odds are excellent that the person protecting his BMW was the same race as the dead loser. Otherwise, we would still be hearing about the racist tragedy of it all because the carjacker was surely just about to "turn his life around" and become a cardiologist.

The gun grabbing by the Nazis and the Communists and how that turned out is well documented. But what about the countries that have knuckled under more recently? The Aussies are a tough and admirable people, but they have neither the same constitutional protection nor history as we do. They allowed themselves, at least on paper, to be disarmed. Not here. Not ever. The grandstanding little Attention Hoggs, the pandering politicians, the pint-sized billionaire soda scold who heaped scorn and criticism upon the Texas church hero, will not prevail. Pass all the laws you want restricting our sacred constitutional right to keep and bear arms. Law enforcement will not enforce; gun owners will not comply.

The Canadians are now and always have been willing accomplices in their own serfdom. Face it – their forebears were the ones loyal to the King George Monarchy who preferred to flee rather than fight for liberty. "Life, liberty, and the pursuit of happiness" is the motto of a free people. "Knuckling under, saying what we're told to say, and electing soy boys in blackface," not so much. I'm sorry; my bad. The correct motto – and what a rallying cry it is! – is "From sea to sea."

Now I hasten to add that I have met very few Canadians whom I haven't liked personally. Except for being embarrassing tippers, most are hale fellows, well met, extremely nice, and in our gated community, solid and impressive partiers, any one of whom could drink me under the table.
Our Canadian neighbors fought very bravely in the World Wars. Since then…it's been a long slog toward politically correct serfdom while often maintaining a pathetic kind of fetish, when abroad, to make sure that everyone knows they are not – icky poo – Americans. Even as they count on us when they desperately need to jump the queue to get decent and timely medical care, or to spend the winter in our more pleasant southern climes.

Once a couple of decades ago, I entertained at a corporate Christmas Party in Winnipeg, after which the emcee warned people to go to their cars in groups because the night before, three people had been robbed at knifepoint. At first, I honestly thought the emcee was joking.

I was impressed by the sheer determination of a lone assailant to venture out in December when Winnipeg was at least ten thousand degrees below zero. That may have been Centigrade, I'm not sure. I do know that it was disconcerting to be anywhere where Minnesota was SOUTH. Plus, all the cars in the parking lot were plugged in to big headbolt heaters during the banquet. Whispers went around the head table that the perpetrator was described by his victims as a First Nations Person who may have been drunk. That piece of information made it yet more unlikely that an inebriated Mr. Stands With A Knife could have located a vital area to stab that wasn't swathed in seven layers of down and fleece.

In America, a knife-wielding jackass would have to worry that he could risk being met by someone with a much better weapon, deadly at a safe distance from his knife.

Congratulations, Virginians, on a beautiful Second Amendment rally. I feel pretty safe from the gun grabbers here in gun-friendly Arizona. But should push come to shove, at least in my neighborhood, it is by no means settled science who would be pushed and what would be shoved and where, Eric Swalwell and his nuclear warheads notwithstanding. Little Green Greta fantasizes about walls for mass execution; Bernie Bots gleefully anticipate gulags; Kathy Griffin favors beheading; but only Eric looks forward to nuking his fellow citizens. What comes after dialing it up to eleven?

NOBODIES

February 14, 2020

When we lived in San Francisco in the early ’70s, an episode of *The Streets of San Francisco* was filmed right outside the front door of our flat. The show featured Karl Malden and a young, hot Michael Douglas. In those halcyon days, the streets of San Francisco were not yet covered in poop, even in our poor working-class and ethnic neighborhood. I rushed outside with my little baby in my arms, hoping to get him into a crowd scene just so I could tell his grandparents to look for it.

Michael Douglas actually spoke to me and told me that it would not work out because the baby was “too fat” for television where the camera adds 10 pounds! He was joking and we both had a good laugh. In point of fact, at three months, my son weighed a hefty 18 pounds and I had dressed him in a little outfit with a blue velvet bow tie which, sadly, could not even be seen under his several chins. Talk about a “wardrobe malfunction”!

Later, when he developed into an extremely beautiful toddler with a mop of blonde curls (I can brag freely because he is a clone of his father), I briefly explored signing him up with a modeling agency for print and advertising work. But I was told that “he really is TOO cute. We are looking for average looking children, so everyone can relate.” Honest to God.

Which brings us to Super Bowl LIV – although somewhat belatedly, as happens with a once a week column — and the gazillion dollar 30 second ads and the half-time spectacle and what I believe it all means.

When I think back on any ads that ever made an impact on me, they are few and far between. Memorable candidates would be the gorgeous Clydesdales in the snow with the jingle bell bridles; “Mikey” the little cereal eater who “doesn’t like anything” yet scarfed down Life Cereal; the great little old lady bellowing “Where’s the beef?”; many of the clever Geico gecko ads, especially Mrs. Lincoln asking poor Honest Abe if her dress made her look fat; and the greatest ad campaign of all time, the E-Trade Babies Series. There was wit, style, cleverness to all of those. Heck, as a kid I even liked the dancing Hamm’s bear. “From the land of sky blue waaaaters…Hamm’s the beer refreshing!” Very catchy tune.

This Super Bowl crop of ads was the most boring, the most obnoxious, the least clever bunch of sad offerings in my lifetime. And what was the unifying theme of every last one of them? Celebrities! Celebrities! Celebrities! And more celebrities! Takeaway lesson: “If you ain’t a celebrity, you ain’t squat.”

We have now come full circle from ad agencies wanting an “everyman” look, an “average” baby, to Only The Beautiful People Need Apply. We will train you to wear what they wear, drive what they drive, but most importantly of all, to think the same political drivel they spew.

In case we didn’t “get” it right out of the chute, the Mostly Naked Ladies high up on stage were being virtually worshipped by the crowd below. Oh yes, as the cherry on top of this frothy Schiff sundae, the kids with their little arms in the air “reaching for the Stars” were in bizarre cages. Get it? It’s just like the (Obama-era) cages of children separated for their own safety from detained illegal invaders who may or may not be related in any way to the children. All I could think of as I kept watching the Chyron of Super Bowl LIV, was that “LIV” is 54 in Roman Numerals, but it is also the abbreviation for Low Information Voters. At whom this Super Bowl halftime waste of money was aimed.

I confess that I am also "Low Information" when it comes to RECOGNIZING celebrities. Since I do not go to movies or watch television, celebrity worship is wasted on me. My knowledge level consists of saying, "I think that is one of the unfunny late-night Jimmies, no idea which one." I did enjoy the Bill Murray *Groundhog Day* homage which is a perfect metaphor for everything the Democrat Party has done for the last 3 years, except without the uplifting moral of the movie in which the cynical Murray finally learns to be a better person.

A fair amount has been written about the skanky half-time show. I think Jennifer Lopez is a beautiful woman and we were left with no doubt that she must work out for many hours a day to maintain that level of fitness at 50. But, whatever that was, it was not dancing. Yeah, yeah, okay, Boomer. I love actual dance of all kinds – ballet, tap, modern, ballroom – and regularly play the fabulous YouTube compilation of real dancing set to Uptown Funk. Fred Astaire, Gene Kelly, the insanely-talented Nicholas Brothers, and many others perform world-class dance moves without a single hypersexualized aerobic pole dancer among them.

And yes, this first-levy Boomer knows that the waltz was once considered skanky. But there was nothing uplifting, creative, or lovely in all the silly twerking, jerking and grabbing on that stage. Not even to mention trying to shoehorn some tedious political points into it.

I do not think women belong in chadors. Nor do I care what women are willing to flaunt for money and fame, from icky sex tapes to "adult" films to entire outfits that could be carried in a Sandwich Baggie. Not my bidness; not my problem. But fall for it at your own risk, fellas.

What does terrify me is the stunning hypocrisy of the feminninnies in calling objections to such behavior "slut shaming" (a bad thing) while simultaneously retaining the power to fire, expel, or sue any male who actually RESPONDS to it! The campuses and "woke" corporate workplaces are basically little more than honey traps. "Look at me in this skimpy outfit!" screams the half-time show. "Don't you DARE look or you will lose your scholarship and your job and maybe even go to jail!" shriek the power-mad Professional Grievance Grubbers. You may say that is "sending a mixed message." I don't think there is anything "mixed" about it – it is deliberate, it is dishonest, and it is as deadly to men as a Black Widow is to her mate.

The whole celebrity ad tsunami made me think of the Emily Dickinson poem: "I'm nobody! Who are you? Are you nobody too? Then there's a pair of us — don't tell; They'd banish us, you know. How dreary to be somebody! How public like a frog. To tell your name the livelong day. To an admiring bog." Dreary, maybe, but very very lucrative and entitled.

The bottom line the celebrity overload was meant to convey: "You are really a nobody. These are the only people who count. Your only hope is to revere them and conform to them." Naturally, the silly, unwatched Oscars continued that theme. Come November, let's show them who counts. Again.

GERIATRIC MULTI-TASKING

February 21, 2020

I just read a semi-depressing article which advised seniors not to attempt multi-tasking. It appears that we are supposed to marshal our meager remaining mental resources to focus like a laser on one task at a time, lest we fall down and hurt ourselves or otherwise start the house on fire. I had come to the same conclusion myself some time ago.

Oh, how the mighty have fallen! Back when Mama and Daddy still lived in the sweet little house I grew up in, and Mama, 90, was sick of cooking, I often made my own version of "Meals on Wheels" wherein I prepared from scratch and froze in small, labeled food savers, 54, count 'em, 54, meals. This included Chili, Spaghetti Sauce, Brisket, two different kinds of Chicken, Bean Soup, Lasagna, Irish Lamb Stew, and Pot Roast and Gravy.

With these freezer treasures alternating with Chicken Pot Pies and going out for Tacos or Chinese they could eat for several months. I would give much of what I own to be able to do that for Mama again even for a week. The point today, however, is not how much I miss my Mother, which is unquantifiable, but how efficiently I managed to make 54 meals in about half a day.

And that was using one stove that had one oven in a kitchen the size of an inadequate walk-in closet. Now, I am blessed with a yuge, dream kitchen, and to make an ordinary breakfast, I need to approach it with military planning, timers and lists. Sigh.

It is a "revoltin' development" indeed (h/t to William Bendix in *Life of Riley*) when the Queen of Deviled Eggs in the

Dusty Little Village, possibly all of Arizona, puts a dozen eggs on the boil, goes to write a column for many appreciative commenters and a couple of trolls, and does not come back to the kitchen until she hears a fearful popping she thinks is gunfire. And upon viewing the egg parts everywhere, almost wishes it had been gunfire. Now I set the timer with the precision of someone who must take a pill at an exact time or die!

No more freelancing without double-checking recipes, especially when baking. Bread without yeast isn't even matzo. It's a complete waste of ingredients and time. These are not yet frequent occurrences, thank the Lord, but they happen often enough to provide a window into a scary future. I blame the fact that I am so easily distracted, first, on Donald J.Trump, of course, because why not? But also on the fact that I seem to be at a stage in my life where I find almost everything equally fascinating and equally urgent.

So I will go into the garage headed for the Gift Wrapping Bin and see the Gun Cleaning Bench and decide to clean my Walther PPQ. Then I will remember the gift that has to be wrapped and taken to the UPS Store by the close of day and get the scissors out of the Junk Drawer but decide to organize the Junk Drawer before wrapping the gift. If I'm going to the UPS Store, I might as well swing by Fry's, so I have to make out a grocery list, but, oh look at the ridiculous number of ballpoint pens that don't even work, yet are retained for years. Time to try them all out and eliminate the spent ones. I have hundreds, just from hotels alone.

And as sands through the hourglass, these are the Days of My Life.

A dear friend of mine must scour the Internet looking for the most depressing stories to text me with links. Sometimes I do not open them, but often I do. There was one in this same theme, not of problems with multi-tasking for seniors, but with the horrendous projected costs incurred in Assisted Living and caregiving for Seniors. Daunting!

I have an alternative to Assisted Living and that is a Revised Standard Version of THE COMMUNE!! Yes! THIS TIME, like Communism, it will really work. Sure, when you were in your early 20s, you tried communal living, supposedly sharing everything and you ended up putting your initials on your eggs and hiding anything of value from the listless, lazy, thieving roommates sharing your filthy living space. (Naturally, Bernie Sanders lived in a commune in the '60s and was thrown out for preferring to BS rather than work. Shocked, I am.)

But we have all matured and now have mad skills. Plus money. By the time we need Assisted Living in another 10-15 years, the cost for one person in Assisted Living is projected to be well over $100,000 each year, every year, except when it goes UP. Krikey! Multiply that times ten to 12, say, and we could build a darn fine 8-bedroom house in rural Arizona with at least 12 bathrooms and both private areas and some nice common areas inside and out.

Who wants in on Ammoville Acres, Phase One? We're going to need somebody who's a doctor or nurse. Somebody who is a lawyer would always come in handy. One or more Tech People. A phone wizard who will help me forward a picture. Excellent marksmen for our security force. We can hire cleaning and yard work done, but home handyman skills will be much prized, as well as the ability to drive at night.

I will volunteer right now to cook and tell jokes. I hope our friend Margie joins to be the baker and both her husband, Don, and my bestie, Angela, know how to farm should that become necessary if any Democrat ever gets in again and destroys the economy, as they all promise. Since I don't do so well with houseplants, I have a sneaking suspicion that farming is not quite as easy as Mike the Tyke says it is. Especially corn in Arizona, corn being Mike's area of massive agricultural expertise.

We would have a dozen people to help somebody remember the name of that actress who was in that series about some town in South Dakota. Right now, just being married and having two half brains helps reconstruct and retrieve some information, but think of the benefits of having 12 people to yell out the answers on Jeopardy.

We could rent stretch limos to take us to concerts with Willie Nelson, the Eagles, or the Rolling Stones, who will all still be performing. We could order groceries online and have them delivered, and put up a revolving Duty List to keep everything neat and squared away. There should surely be no more disagreements than the average HOA meeting and the common areas could be Gun-Free Zones during Policy Meetings.

So that's my idea, folks. Now taking applications to get in on the ground floor. Please include skills, resources, preferred pronouns – Her Big Fat Royal Majesty is already taken — dietary restrictions, and pictures. Recent pictures. Not like the one for this column. I kid, of course. Skills are MUCH more important than pictures! But attractiveness is never unwelcome; studies have been done – even babies and animals prefer pretty people.

Figures!

THE BIG CHILL

February 28, 2020

The Press has long been called "The Fourth Estate," a term that comes to us from pre-revolutionary French history. (The First Estate was the King and nobility; the Second Estate was the Church; and the Third Estate was the "commoners." Because of the power of the press, at some point it was designated as The Fourth Estate.) When the felicitous term migrated to the United States, it was originally deemed critical that The Fourth Estate be above the fray, an independent and unbiased institution. (Stop laughing…)

The institution – electronic, print and social media — has decided in the last few decades to have the kind of Estate Sale that one reads about in the papers. Sold! Lock, stock, and barrel to the far left-wing of the Democrat Party for invitations to the best DC parties, occasional sex for a leak leading to a scoop, and obscene salaries for reading aloud. For the first few years of the shredding of its Unbiased Mission Statement, an effort was made to be a little bit stealthy about it. But shortly after Donald J. Trump descended that escalator and declared himself a candidate for the Presidency, the veil dropped. National Coming Out Day for the Media was proudly declared. No more "who, what, when, where, why" with even a thin veneer of objectivity. It was "all hands on deck to screw over Orange Man Bad."

Nothing good, nothing positive, nothing humanizing must EVER get through! Under no circumstances should DJT be "normalized." They actually used that word. So far beyond the pale was this President, this human being, that every single thing he touched had to be attacked – his dessert, how he likes his steak, his beautiful wife, her Christmas decorations, the First Lady's clothes, her shoes, yes, even her ACCENT, for pity's sake, never mind that she speaks five languages and most of the newsheads are semi-literate in one. The President is not only "literally" Hitler but also a Russian agent which is a good trick. And – talk about the pudgy pot calling the kettle fat – David "Pretend Republican" Frum says that Trump is our fattest President ever. Can you even imagine that shameless, rotund little Frump calling out, say, Stacy Abrams, for her weight?

That is bad enough. But it doesn't end there. In addition to tedious hourly ATTACKS on the President, the media giants DECIDE what is and what is not news.

This can happen by simple omission: "Let's see – here's a story about MS-13 illegals raping and killing a young woman (ah, that's just a local crime story, not of general interest, bad for The Narrative...). Here's a story about Ilhan Omar being married to her brother – oh, that's been DEBUNKED, and bad for The Narrative. Wait, here's a story where Trump said 40,000 people were at a rally when it was only 39,400. Let's go with: Trump Lies Again!"

Are we done yet? No, we are not. The final step in the Estate Sale treachery is to BECOME the story.

This also takes several forms, from making a tedious and argumentative 3-minute statement at a News Conference instead of asking an actual question, to repeating an asked-and-answered question ad infinitum, to ambushing representatives from the Evil Republican Party in hallways and corridors with what they believe are going to be "Gotcha" soundbites on the evening news. Sometimes that can blow up in their arrogant, smirky little faces, and then watch the stuff hit the fan!

Manu Raju is the Senior Congressional Correspondent for an insignificant, unwatched network whose two-fold business plan consists of getting and retaining the franchise to annoy trapped airport travelers and being part of a cable package. He is very full of himself.

As you recall, during the waste of time Impeachment Follies he approached Arizona Senator Martha McSally and asked her if she supported allowing more "witnesses" than the ones the brilliant Democrat strategists had rushed half-baked to the Senate. And Senator McSally blew past him and said: "Manu, you're a liberal hack. I'm not talking to you."

WELL, I NEVER! It's the end of the world as we know it! Manu's media cronies and bosses alike demanded an apology and howled that a Senator's ability to just blow off a hounding little pipsqueak who "identifies" as a journalist was CHILLING!

Oooooh. Chilling! Not that! Anything but that! These hacks – and Martha had that absolutely right — can call us Trump voters ANY damn thing they want. Following the lead of Barack Hussein Obama, they can claim utterly without evidence that we hate and fear "The Other." They can repeat losing loser Hillary's disgusting Deplorable name-calling. They can make fun of our teeth, say we smell, say we didn't graduate from one of them there colleges, attack every value we hold dear. That's all right and proper. High humor to those frat boys.

They are perfectly comfortable smearing every Trump voter as a fascist and a racist (even the black ones, in fact, ESPECIALLY the black ones) and exposing us to attacks in several cities by a roving band of masked arsonists and thugs who can beat people as cops are ordered to stand down. Now THAT should be chilling, even to liberals.

But call THEM "hacks" and they run to their megaphones to explain how terrifying such disrespect is. Why, it could even call down violence upon their lacquered, empty heads. Yeah, right. There has never been an attack on ANYONE by any Trump supporters that I am aware of. Some have successfully DEFENDED themselves from Antifa attacks, a few delightful enough to watch over and over on YouTube. But the only journalist that has ever been harmed was Andy Ngo, in a racist, homophobic attack by the black-shirt Antifas.

To media stars, the single-most narcissistic and entitled profession in my experience – and that includes heavy competition from judges, actors and politicians! — the cold shower of mockery is what is horrific. THAT is something up with which they cannot put.

Finally, talk about CHILLING, as an owner of, let's just call it "several," guns, I'd like to apologize to America for the 150 million Americans who have been killed in the last few years because of my owning these weapons. As a certified lying dog-faced pony soldier, I know I should just believe Biden – and vote for him in his race for Senate – but you'd think someone would have noticed nearly half the population gone. Remember, he's their "moderate" hope, and for eight long years was a heartbeat away from the Presidency. Yikes!

OSCARS SO STUPID

March 6, 2020

Yes. I know that it's March now and the Oscars were last month. But the has-been celebrities continue to attack, so I thought a never-was columnist should fight back.

A few years ago, the Wokest of the Wokesters had serious complaints about the Oscars' lack of black nominees. Several people boycotted and dubbed them #OscarsSoWhite. At no time did any of the complainers indicate exactly which paleface nominees should have been eliminated and which nominees of some other color should have been nominated in their place. But surely the raaacist "fix" had to be in, somehow, someway. Because, reasons.

I probably haven't watched the Oscars for at least twenty years. Usually I had seen one or two of the nominated movies at most. And the dreary speeches kept getting longer and longer and more and more political. And even though for at least a couple of those early years, I probably favored the same politicians and causes as the droning pontificators, I still found it just plain inappropriate in a venue that was supposed to be celebratory, not hectoring. Like most sane people, I have a visceral hatred of being lectured, whether by Joaquin Phoenix or Sasheen Littlefeather.

To save time in future Oscar speechifying, I have compiled a batch of appropriate short speeches on spec. Have no fear, starlets of all genders, about plagiarizing. What do you do, anyway, but memorize dialogue that someone else has written for you?

Separate an actor from a writer and you've got Jussie Smollett writing his own script for a hate crime hoax. Dave Chappelle claimed that even black people didn't buy it. I have tremendous respect for Robin Roberts, but COME ON, MAN! Did she really believe his preposterous tale? Cory Booker, Kamala Harris, sure; but Robin seems both smart and sane.

We've all experienced watching a celebrity flounder on *The Tonight Show*. But.. but… but… that actress plays a smartie-pants in her sitcom! How can she be such a boring dunce? Because she's ACTING. She has large breasts and a pretty face. What was that fetching and wildly-inaccurate turn of phrase Mike the Tyke used about farmers? Oh yeah, they don't need a lot of "grey matter." Heck, without James Woods in the house, the collective IQ at the Oscars was instantly cleaved (cloven?) in half. So, here we go. I submit, as a community service:

THE ANGRY BALD ACTIVIST PRESENTER SPEECH
See what you made me do? I have shaved my head, but not, as you can see, my armpits. As my heroine Greta said: How DARE YOU? How DARE YOU? We have just 8 years, 4 months and 22 days left before it's too late to save Gaia, our Earth Mother, even though I am totally pro-choice on Motherhood. So if Mother Earth wants to abort us all, well, that's cool. Fat people, who should nevertheless not be body shamed, are drinking 64 ounce Big Gulps and wearing fur. Straws, people! Little children are using straws! Everything is terrible.

(Deep breath, emphasizing cleavage…regaining control): But I have a job to do here. Soooo…The 5 nominees for Best Picture of the Year are: Donald Trump, Satanic Putin-Loving Hitler; Diverse Scrawny Women with One Fat One Save The World; Diverse Scrawny Women with One Fat One Fight Climate Change; Diverse Scrawny Women with one Fat One Bust Ghosts, and De'LaJa'Queene Bond, Transgender Black Lesbian 007.

THE DERANGED, SHORT, ELDERLY TOUGH GUY PRESENTER DIATRIBE

Eff Trump. (Expect wild applause). No, really, Eff Trump. I would like to eff Trump and throw poo in his face and dump wee-wee on his head and shoot him and behead him and stab him. Because Hitler. Literally Hitler. Never mind that Hitler is literally dead. Never mind that I don't know what "literally" means. I want to take Trump out behind the barn and open a big can o' whup-ass upon him and …I see some insignificant nobody is waving a sign, trying to tell me my time is up. God, these lift shoes are killing me – how DO women walk in heels? Now I don't have time to read the nominees for Best Actor. Their names have been in all the trades anyway. Hey, remember, it's an honor just to be nominated. Just eff Trump. That's the important thing.

THE YOUNG FEMI-NINNY ACCEPTANCE SPEECH

Oh my God, you guys. I never expected I would beat all those other women pretending to smile right now. Sisters! We ALL won, even though, technically, I am the one with the Oscar and you are not. I would like to thank everyone – you know who you are, it's hardly important to mention you by name, as my time here is so limited by sexism and white supremacy – but everyone who gave me the opportunity to play this important award-winning role in this brave and important movie. It was, like, about something brave and empowering and courageous and important with women, women, women of every color and gender in it. Who cares if nobody went to it? The important thing was, like, you know, the courage. And my award.

It was, like, totally worth killing a baby to win this award. (Expect standing ovation.)

THE OLD FEMI-NINNY PRESENTER SPEECH

There are no good roles for women over 23 and I never once objected to this back when I could pass for 23. But now I am

53, uh, 53-ish, and I feel it is of profound importance to mention the lack of roles for older women who still have giant pouty lips and perky, if rock solid breasts. I have chosen to wear this cape I had my housekeeper, Maria, embroider. No, wait, she quit; it was Luz or Lupe, whatever. The cape displays the names of some women directors you have never heard of to show how hip I am. Sure, I have never used a woman director when I have had anything to say about it, because then I wouldn't be the Queen Bee on the set. But, hey, the cape! Look at me making a statement! Just LOOK AT ME!! I have eaten nothing but kale for two weeks to fit into this g****** dress! Stop talking to each other and LOOK AT ME, G**d*&%it!

THE PANTRY PREP QUEEN

March 13, 2020

Okay. I have overstated my Prepping Cred as any kind of royalty by several orders of magnitude. I understand there are religions that advise their adherents to store up to a year's worth of food, and at least one serious prepper I know who not only makes his own ammo (child's play in Prep World), but also has a wide variety of food dehydrators, plus good old-fashioned canning skills, multiple generators, water purifiers and the like. I bow low.

Nevertheless, when there is a chance that my family may be asked to isolate itself for several weeks, I want to be ready to do that. So I have done quite a bit of preparation beyond my normal OCD levels.

First of all, I figure with my incredibly slow metabolism (picture a car that could go from coast to coast burning but one gallon of gas…), I could probably live for most of those weeks just on water and the occasional doughnut for morale and still only lose five pounds. So I got that goin' for me, which is nice. I can give almost all our stored food to Mr. AG who is a foot taller and whose metabolism burns through probably 6,000 calories a day, no problem. As I write this, he has just consumed five Hebrew National Hot Dogs, two baked potatoes, sauerkraut and two bananas. Also 3 chocolates and a granola bar. And that's what I know about.

Secondly, I have more than a touch of agoraphobia – odd for a comedian, but perfect for a columnist – and was born to be under either quarantine or house arrest for an indefinite period of time! As a bookish child with minimal social skills, I used to dream of being locked in the public library for several years. The fantasy was vague on important details like food.

The highlights of the daydream were simply that there would be no school, no old-maid teachers, several of them psychotic enough to make Hillary and Elizabeth Warren seem almost pleasant, and books as far as the eye could see. Heaven on earth!

You know how when some guy goes off the rails, the "journalists" always interview his surviving neighbors, most of whom swear that "he was a quiet guy, kept to himself, seemed nice enough, this was totally unexpected"? Well, I think I was odd enough that my neighbors would not have been all that surprised.

"Uh, listen, her parents were great. But she used to go into the nearby swamp alone and write poetry. She did not like to play with the other children; she liked to READ! Sometimes she wrote little skits and put them on in the backyard and she once started a newspaper, each copy written by hand and sold it door to door. Just a very strange little girl..."

Had I not met my twin besties in ninth grade, who (miracle of miracles!) also liked to read, and then met my *bashert* (my fated beloved) as a teenager, I might still be working on my 72-page single spaced Manifesto, wearing a hoodie and sunglasses.

Thirdly, ALREADY, long before the COVID-19 Panic, I had a dread fear of not being able to feed my loved ones. Once in San Francisco when our son was a baby, there was some sort of long-forgotten dairy panic and all the milk disappeared from the shelves of the grocery stores. Or at least the one I could walk to since we didn't own a car.

One barefooted dirty hippie girl had just finished loading all twelve remaining gallons into her cart. I said, "Look, I have a six-month old. I breast-feed him, but I need the milk for me to make the milk. May I please have just one? You will still have eleven." She refused. She said she didn't even have kids and just planned to scalp it to other desperate people. I said, "Well, you haven't paid for that yet, so if you are going to be a (several bad words), I will just take one then." And so I did. She screamed in outrage and, frankly, shock, but there were no cameras in stores yet, so what could she do? She briefly considered fighting for it, but thought better of it. I mean, what kind of scary lunatic takes stuff out of another woman's cart? Without so much as a Swiss Army Knife? Better to cut your losses and move on.

Now since that time, I have always had a full pantry that looks like a food shelf warehouse, two fridges and two freezers, and backups to my backups of everything from the newly-scarce toilet paper, to garbage bags to aspirin, vitamins, and laundry detergent.

Here is my plan in the unlikely event that we are quarantined in our Gated Geezerville. First, we will eat what is probably two weeks' worth of lovely prepared meals in the freezer – Red Beans and Rice, Moroccan Lamb Stew, Short Ribs, Sloppy Joes, and Turkey-Rice Casserole, to name just a few items. We will eat up all the fresh food in the fridge – various salad fixins, cottage cheese, other kinds of cheese, ice cream, eggs, all the fruits and vegetables. We will eat really well in Phase One, maybe even invite friends over for dinner.

Mr. AG, sadly, will run out of what I call his "Joe-ceries" quite quickly – he eats 3 or 4 bananas a day, so we should hit the Banana Crisis by Day 4 or 5. The Yogurt Depletion would come next. But Potato Chips, Whiskey and Granola Bars will last forever.

I have diced and frozen little bags of onions and peppers. When the fresh vegetables are gone, Mr. AG will raise a glass rather than complain. Given the choice between broccoli and death, he would have to channel the great Jack Benny line, "I'm thinking; I'm thinking!"

If we still can't get to a market safely when all that is gone, we move to the Involuntary Vegan Stage – staples like rice, beans, kasha, quinoa (a trendy ancient grain supposedly good for you), nuts, pastas, oatmeal, cereal, grits, and soup. I have a bread machine and am not afraid to use it. We have tuna to last several monotonous weeks.

Weeks 6-8 would entail the challenging Freestyle Phase – things like Lima Bean, Salsa, and Cheezit Surprise; my grandson's leftover CapNCrunchberries cereal with Almond Milk; Aunt Lucy's gift fruitcake (Aunt Lucy died in 1997) and Gefiltefish (think fish SPAM) with Water Chestnuts, Craisins and Dill Pickles. Pretty much anything left with a calorie in it. I expect by this phase, what with being locked in the house with each other and God forbid, running low on coffee or butter, that an active bartering system could arise with neighbors. "Will trade Vintage 2017 Canned Beets for a banana" will probably not win the day.

Well, speaking of hoarding, gotta run to my gun store to check out the new AR-14 Joe Biden spoke of at the auto plant. He also argued that nobody "needed" 100 rounds of ammo. Oh my. If that's 9 mm, the idiot is talking about ONE BOX. Gone in maybe 15 minutes at the range. Twenty-some "contendas" in the Dem primary and this is what is left. Well done, Democrats, you must be so proud!

THE WOEFUL WUHAN BLUES

March 20, 2020

Last week, when I thought we were talking about 14 days of voluntary quarantining, I outlined how I was prepared to live on what I had in my freezer and pantry for six to eight weeks. That still seems pretty accurate. And then my President blurted out that this could continue until late summer or early fall! Quoi? The stock market went into freefall and the grocery store parking lots filled up like my ankles in the eighth month of pregnancy.

On Monday, I UPSed twelve rolls of toilet paper to my son and his family in St. Paul, MN. My son had been on a two-day quest to find extra rolls and he had returned home as despondent as a deer hunter who had failed to bag his 10-point buck. My beautiful and creative daughter-in-law says she knows how to make paper and she will soon turn her superpowers to the manufacture of boutique toilet paper. Like Gloria Gaynor, "We Will Survive"!

I ventured into my local Bashas grocery store which resembled either Venezuela or a 7-11 Store in Florida when a hurricane is already at Cat 5. The shoppers looked like they were on a festive field trip from an insane asylum – many wearing colorful long-sleeved rubber gloves, dousing themselves in sanitizer after putting each item in their baskets. Mind you, in the entire state of Arizona – not one of your smaller states geographically — as of this writing, there were 20 people with COVID-19, 5 in one family, and no deaths. That's no, none, nada, bupkis. We were probably all in much graver danger from the plague of wrong-way drivers in AZ than from the COVID-19 plague. Not that I don't take this all seriously.

Every paper good that could possibly be pressed into service as toilet tissue was gone, including paper towels, napkins, and The Arizona Republic. From there, the choices frantic consumers were making struck me as somewhat random and whimsical. All the eggs were gone; all the potatoes were gone; most meat was gone and canned goods were seriously picked over. The "Asian and Hispanic" aisle was as bare as a Code Pink fattie protesting whatever gave xer the excuse to flop around naked again.

The only tortillas in sight were either gluten-free, whole wheat, or made of some inappropriate ingredients like spinach or garbanzo beans. And there were darn few even of those.

By some miracle, I found every single item I sought on this trip! A couple cleaning products, precious green bananas, a loaf of bread, yogurt and cottage cheese. And later, at Walmart, two forty-pound bags of softener salt.

Evidently, the motto of my fellow Arizonans is "Death by Starvation Before Turkey Bacon," so I loaded up on three pounds of it. Sure it tastes like Bandaids, but if you crisp it enough in olive oil it is almost edible. After several decades, we are used to it. Hebrew National Hot Dogs sat alone on their shelf and called my name.

To my surprise, fresh fruits and vegetables were well stocked, except for the aforementioned potatoes. The shoppers sprinted right past the broccoli, asparagus and arugula. Maybe because fresh food wouldn't last long enough for the grimly determined shoppers' purposes. And maybe because it turns out people like Mashed Potatoes better than Mashed Cauliflower, never mind that they are both white. It's fooling nobody. One is a creamy delicious treat and one a hideous disappointment.

Stuff with an expiration date well into next year was much prized and one young (by my standards) man was near-orgasmic to find three large cans of Chef Boyardee Spaghetti and Meatballs. (Talk about a product that can make Turkey Bacon seem delish by comparison!)

Bread flour sat on the shelf, as did many things from which a cook can make other things. Evidently, many people cannot or do not wish to cook and rely almost exclusively on fast food, canned food, and mixes. I feel well suited to this kind of an ordeal for two reasons: one, cooking is one of my six discernible skills; and two, I know how to "be poor" and thank God for that.

Some people -- my dear late mother comes to mind — are born poor and struggle mightily to overcome. But my husband and I were both born into the solid middle class and, through a variety of stupid life decisions (not even including substance abuse), managed to ACHIEVE near-poverty for many of our early years! It's great training for going through tough times. And makes you really appreciate your re-entry into the middle class.

The Holiest Day of the Jewish Year is The Day of Atonement – Yom Kippur. It is a Fast Day (oh, it's not "Fast" in the sense of SPEEDY; it lasts nearly forever), rather, it is a day of reflection and self-denial in which, for 25 hours, the penitent has no food or water. I mention it because our Minnesota synagogue had a custom of donating the equivalent of what we would have eaten in three meals to the food shelves. A huge semi was parked in front of the synagogue from Second Harvest, and routinely loaded several TONS of food for the poor from our 750 families of congregants. But one of the caveats we got every year was that the food had to be virtually instant, with minimal reading of directions for preparation. Sad.

So, Wuhan Blues, Week One is in the can with very little difference in my life so far. However, once we get to go to a restaurant again, I am going to leave a spectacular tip in wild appreciation. Max Cossack, famous novelist, is about to notice the difference big time as our Gated Geezerville has closed until further notice the entire clubhouse which includes the outdoor pool and his gym. I offered to locate the 10-lb dumbbells I bought with misplaced optimism after my shoulder injury and he just looked at me. “Honey, I do curls with 80 lbs of weight, and even that is not very impressive for a man.” Oh. Well then we won’t even mention my 5-lb weights. In my defense, I do 4 sets of 14 reps three times a week. That has to count for something, doesn’t it? As in “better than nothing?” At 73? I just want to continue to be able to rack my slide.

Well, if we can’t go to bars or restaurants, every conceivable entertainment is cancelled, how to put a little joy into the next several weeks? I baked several loaves of challah (braided sweet bread for the Sabbath) and also made a Coconut Cream Pie. I think I will make a pie or a cake a week and see if I can’t gain another 10 pounds, just in case this pestilence really does last until – are you KIDDING, Mr. President?? – SEPTEMBER?

While others fight over the Charmin, and shower in Purell, I will be the smart one storing up fat for the long haul. You can’t be too careful. Who’s WITH me???

WORSENING WUHAN WOES

March 27, 2020

Okay, you guys. Sure, some 50,000 Americans got sick since last we spoke. Sure, several hundred souls who somebody loved have passed away. My heart breaks for all of them. I am praying for Amy Klobuchar's husband's complete recovery. None of this is a laughing matter. Still, lightening your load with humor is my mission, so what can I do?

BECAUSE NOW IT'S GETTING SERIOUS: I HAVE TO DO MY OWN HOUSEWORK!!

My housekeeper lives in Phoenix, almost an hour away from the Dusty Little Village, and, of course, she has other clients as well. It just didn't make any sense while we were sheltering in place to have her come into the house, though she is a very smart, clean and careful person. (Put away your stupid Race Cards, lefties; no, I am not afraid of a Mexican woman. It's her other clients I am worried about, all as white as the driven snow.)

And although I am not a multi-multi-billionaire like some lying welshers who don't keep their promises to their employees, I am continuing to pay her anyway. I love her like a daughter. I know a lot of employees are hurting, while the despicable Democrats dither, carp, and delay, but my employee will not be one of them. Heck, that money is in my budget anyway, the only difference will be that I will have to get off my dead behind to do an inferior job of what she does every week. I am eternally grateful.

It has been a long time since I have cleaned my own house and I do not enjoy it. I string out all week what it takes my housekeeper about 3 hours to do. Sad. It's not that it's beneath me. My own mother cleaned others' houses for decades. It's just that it's beyond me.

I used to use this line in my act to great effect: "Being on the road so much, I now have a professional housecleaner. It was my husband's idea. One day he up and declared, 'No wife of mine is going to clean toilets.' Actually it was more of an observation than a declaration."

One thing I continue to pride myself on is that I have had no need to fight the crazy crowds in the grocery stores, except to pick up minor incidentals and as an observer. It has been quite the culinary adventure to see how many freezer treasures of uncertain provenance have been unearthed in both freezers. If the 3 most important things in real estate are "location, location, location," the 3 most important things in freezing food are "label, label, label." If you are over 60, do not rely on "Oh, surely I will remember what is in this red food saver."

An answer to the simple question "What's for dinner?" that begins with "Well, it's EITHER…" is not going to end well.

"What's your best guess?"

"Either Turkey Tetrazzini or Chicken Curry. I'll know more when it thaws completely. What's the difference, you like both?"

Sometimes with small children and ADD husbands, you can go for distraction: "But, look what ELSE I found: Chocolate Cake!!"

"It says Happy 70th Birthday on it. If it's yours, it's over three years old. If it's your father's, it's a quarter of a century old."

"Well, it can't be Daddy's. We've only lived here for 10 years. Let's cover it in this warm Vanilla Bourbon Sauce I just made. It won't hardly be dry at all. Hope I didn't overdo the bourbon."

Speaking of Daddy, I think he is a good metaphor for what I believe will happen in the near future. When Daddy turned 70, he was diagnosed with both diabetes and prostate cancer. Naturally, he was scared pretty straight. The nurses gave him a strict diet and told him to lay off sugar, which had been a major part of his diet, and he stuck to his new regimen religiously.

For about six months. Then one day, the whole gathered family was celebrating Mama's birthday in our favorite local restaurant in Alexandria and a bunch of people ordered pie for dessert. Even with Mama giving him the Church Lady pursed-lips treatment, he ordered a piece for himself – Pecan – only the most sugar-intense choice he could have made.

And he didn't die. Not then. Not later. That fact was duly noted, and, quite quickly, he ate whatever the heck he felt like. As regular readers know, he is alive and on his way to 95. His eyesight is decent for a codger, and he has lost no limbs, or even digits, thank the Lord.

He has some memory lapses, mostly involving his uncertain grasp of what era he is in (the Navy? Managing his drugstore? Back in his home in South Dakota?) but he tracks current events very well, and would still make a more reliable presidential candidate than Joe Biden who is 18 years his junior. (Luckily, the prostate cancer turned out to be very non-aggressive and his doc assured him "You'll die WITH this, not OF it. Something else will kill ya." Which seemed to comfort him.)

So all us good little Social Distancers have been isolated and washing our hands to a fare-thee-well, and watching our economy circle the drain.

But one day, like Daddy's big Pie Experiment, some people will get together for an evening of drinking and poker, and nobody will get sick. And eventually, people will conclude that the odds are in their favor.

Hey, remember when we were all young and poor and most of our parties were BYOB, and the bottles people brought were Boone's Farm Apple Wine, the cheapest rotgut rum or whiskey, or, if really splurging, Gallo Spanada arranged elegantly in a punch bowl with sliced citrus fruit? Quelle sophisticated! Well, now we are old and "comfortable," fully stocked with top-shelf brands of every booze known to man. So we no longer host BYOB parties. The party host provides all the liquor and probably some nice hors d'oeuvres as well, or at least several kinds of chips and dips.

But I bet for at least a time, parties will be BYOTP. Stay well, friends.

THE COLUMN TURNS SIX

April 3, 2020

Well, friends, it's that time of year again. March has ended. And good riddance to it. Which means I have been writing *Thoughts From the Ammo Line* for six years. How remarkable that we all look exactly the same as when I started six years ago. At least that's what your avatars indicate, and what MY mirror says when I threaten it with a .45.

Yes, it has now been SIX YEARS since I sent that first (much-shorter) little column to my friend Scott Johnson to see if he might be interested in a conservative Arizona woman's take on guns. And stuff. He was.

And, just like that, I had abandoned my carefree retirement and signed myself up to produce a reasonably humorous, sometimes a teensy bit angry, opinion piece to turn in every single Wednesday morning, ostensibly for the rest of my life! How hard could that be, I thought? Harder than it looks, I found. One of the Guiding Principles of my Life is: "EVERYTHING, no really, EVERYTHING is harder than it looks." Even FARMING! Who knew?

This column right here, right now, is #312, not counting a couple Extra Editions such as the one where Donald J. Trump pulled off the Upset of the Century and rather badly beat Hillary Rodham Clinton for the Presidency of the United States. Perhaps you heard about it? It was all over the news… That happened on a Tuesday, not a Friday, so I got to have a two-fer week. The shocking election was one of the highlights of my life, right up there with my marriage, the birth of my baby, and the Twins winning the 1987 World Series.

And like the Twins winning the 1991 World Series, the 2020 reelection of Donald J. Trump will be sweet, very sweet, especially after the rollicking recovery from the Wuhan Woes. But not QUITE as shocking and wonderful as the first time. We humans are like that: something miraculous and wonderful happens and we are thrilled right up to that moment when we take it for granted and it comes to be expected rather than miraculous. Like the miracle of toilet paper you could buy right off the shelves. Or the ability to welcome friends to your home with a hug. Or even just a handshake. Amazing how much I miss that.

Taking miracles for granted has been ever thus and recorded for all time in the Torah/Holy Bible. "Hey, look at that water from the rock and that manna that has appeared to feed us in the barren desert!" (A "sheltering in place" that lasted for forty years…so quit whining!)

And then, very quickly, "Manna AGAIN? Where are the cucumbers and onions we loved back in Egypt when we were slaves? Man, I sort of miss slavery…" And so on…

In fact, not to borrow trouble, but just wait till the end of President Trump's SECOND term, when the fickle short-attention span electorate will be TIRED of full employment after the economic divorce from China, tired of energy independence and a booming economy that lifts all boats. Mark my words, people will be whining for the "cucumbers" of free college and free medical care and free housing and free food, because who wants all this responsibility and WORKING to get stuff when you can whine or riot until you get it for free or just take it from the people who did work for it?

Unless we believe Bette Midler, brilliant political thinker, who is certain that Trump will rule until he is dead or we are dead or both, up to and including 90,000 years. I'm sorry I will probably not be alive for even half of that 90,000-year run, but it should be an interesting one. Krikey, I didn't even think we had NINETY years left, let alone 90,000. I thought we had fewer than ten, which is why I have given up dieting and flossing and taken up smoking again.

Hundreds of lesser prophets only believe that DJT will demand a third or fourth term, as they confidently predicted would happen with Nixon, Reagan, and "W" Bush. What do all these fellas who were NEVER going to leave their Presidential gig have in common? C'mon, think! Here's a hint: they were all from the exact same Party which we had it on good authority was preparing concentration camps and also going to outlaw birth control for women! Yes, they were evil, Hitleresque, war-on-women, racist Republicans who any minute were going to make women wear unattractive bonnets, because if there's one thing a sex-crazed toxic male loves, it's a woman in a long shapeless dress and a bonnet! And not one of those pathetic imitation Hitlers seized power and stayed on past his eight years.

But back to the six-year anniversary of the column. One of the most embarrassing things that happened to me as a young person – there are sooo many to choose from – involved a tape-recorded Christmas carol for a pageant. It was in fifth grade and I was the only child in the group who knew how to sing harmony. So they stuck me right near the microphone and told me to sing loudly while all the other kids in the group sang melody.

And when they played it back, there was "Silent Night" with one booming alto voice belting out the harmony a third below the melody like Ethel Freakin' Merman. Even the choir director could not help doubling over with laughter. They moved me to the back row and tried again. I learned at a young age that it is not true that you can die of embarrassment, but of course, that was decades before the Internet when things could go viral and hang around forever.

Anyway, that's how I think of the column. Without the commenters, I'm just singing the alto part of a tune. I crank 'em out, tinkering with them right up to the minute I hit "Send," and usually am fairly happy with the work and anxious to get it out there.

And then come the parts that flesh it out – the inveterate punsters, the great memes and cartoons, the heart-warming sharing, the brilliant legal discussions, the back-and-forth between vets of our military branches, the occasional correction – oh, never fear, get something wrong and somebody WILL notice, especially about movie quotes or guns! – the civil disagreements, the camaraderie and really, sense of "family" among people we've never met. And it's just plain FUN. Many kind readers say the column kicks off their weekend on a cheery, uplifting note. Well, dear readers, YOU make MY Friday every single week. I love you guys! Thank you, and thanks, of course, to the Power Line boys for the platform.

And now, finally, I am "caught up" in making compilation books out of each year's collection of columns. The new one, covering April 2019 right up to today is called *Ammo Grrrll Reloads* and will be up on Amazon within a short time. Fear not, I will remind you. I may delay until the Wuhan Worries have mostly abated and your portfolios have rebounded! Thanks so much for buying it and reviewing it with five stars on Amazon. Except for the occasional spell-binding new novel by Max Cossack, I won't be promoting anything else for a whole year!

AFTERWORD

Neither Bette Midler nor Nostradamus could have possibly predicted how 2020 began or ended and what senile klepto-crat is now titularly "in charge" of our fragile Republic, not to mention the Nuclear Codes. Since that disaster and all that led up to it will be the subject of 52 columns in Volume 7 "Ammo Grrrll Gets (a) Shot", I will just say thanks a million for buying this book and go outside and watch another gor-geous Arizona sunset on the patio where my hummingbird Mama is once again sitting on her nest. Humanity has been through much worse and survived. Please, God.

Susan Vass, April 2, 2021